Rseasons ON A RANCH

Rseasons ON A Ranch

*CYNTHIA VANNOY-RHOADES

Authors Choice Press
San Jose New York Lincoln Shanghai

Authors Choice Press
an imprint of iUniverse.com, Inc.

For information address:
iUniverse.com, Inc.
5220 S 16th, Ste. 200
Lincoln, NE 68512
www.iuniverse.com

Originally published by Pruett

ISBN: 0-595-16851-5
Printed in the United States of America

CONTENTS

INTRODUCTION

Someday, ranching as I know it will be gone. It will go the way of the trail herds of the 1800s and the sprawling grasslands of the cattle barons.

Agricultural land is being squeezed out in favor of industry and the "public good." Mining, oil exploration, and urban sprawl are encroaching on this last little piece of the Old West. Someday, this story may be all that's left of a way of life that much of the world will never know.

And ranching is a way of life; it's not just a job. I have been a rancher for fifteen years, as were my father and grandfather before me. From the time I was old enough to ride, I went along with the men to gather cattle, and I helped at the brandings. By the time I was nine I had my own horse, not just one of the ranch horses I had previously ridden. I have always been grateful to my mother, who allowed me to be the tomboy I wanted to be instead of turning me into a lady. All I wanted out of life was to be thought of as a good hand, doing a good job.

Although I have, at times, worked at other jobs, ranching is my life, and the only life I care to live. I love the freedom of galloping across the prairie on a favorite horse; I love fighting the cold, snowy winter to haul feed to hungry cattle; I love being able to bring a half-starved calf back to life.

The feel of the rain, when the summer sun has dried the grass to tiny, brown curls and shrunken water holes to a muddy waste, the wild freedom of riding in a raging windstorm, and the discomfort of riding in a blizzard are all a part of this narrative. They are my own experiences, and you are invited to join me in them. I hope you can feel the cold winds and the hot sun; hear the nighthawks and the meadowlarks; see the early morning sun and smell the rain.

This book is not meant to be a scholarly approach to ranching. It is merely a journey through the seasons on a working ranch that has been in my family for sixty-five years, the U Milliron Cattle Company in northern Wyoming. Come along.

SPRING

I CAN SMELL SPRING IN THE air today. Although it is only March, there is the smell of pine trees in the air. The wind must be blowing down off the Big Horn Mountains to the west of us to smell that good.

My young heifers are already heavy bagged, and two have already calved. The heifers are bred to calve before the rest of the herd so the calves can be weaned earlier and let the mothers grow an extra month or two, and so we can watch the heifers closer for any calving problems.

By the end of March, the older cows will start calving, and we should see tiny, whitefaced calves come into the feed grounds with their mothers.

The hay is in short supply now, and the snow still hasn't started to melt. Dad says we'll have to increase the feed of grain cake and set out more mineral tubs to supplement the dry grasses until the spring green coats the hills. Mineral tubs are made of a mixture of grain, molasses, vitamins, and minerals formulated to give cattle extra energy when the grass is short or dry.

It is still cold outside, and March 21, the first day of spring, looks more

like winter than spring. The snow is still deep and drifted.

The wind is coming up, and snow starts to fall, big, white flakes, wet and heavy. They swirl and dance in front of the wind and soon obscure the landscape. The radio predicted a winter storm for two days ago, and this must be it. It's a little late getting here.

My calves are out in the pasture with their mothers, but I'd better shut them in the corral where they can go under the open shed for shelter. Moving before the wind and snow, the cattle could drift into the half-frozen creek and drown.

The wind whips the snow in my face, and the force of it pushes me back, making me fight my way to the barn and corrals. I can't see my cattle through the storm, even though their black bodies should stand out against the whiteness. Maybe the cows are already in the shed, waiting for the storm to blow over.

In the dark shed, the forms of the five cows and two calves are barely visible, but they are there. The gentle one comes out when she sees me, knowing I will feed her some cake. She will calve next month. I go into the barn, blinding myself for a moment when I turn on the electric light, and pour some grain cake from the sack into a bucket. The five cows crowd around me in the corral, and I scatter the chunks of cake out on the frozen ground. They have plenty of hay, so I shut the gate, although I doubt they will wander outside this late in the day.

Watching the snow, I worry about the calves born out on the range. Spring storms like this are hard on young livestock. The heavy, wet snow and the freezing temperatures create a chill situation that their young bodies are not equipped to handle. The calf's short, thin hair is quickly soaked through, and unless he can be brought into a warm, dry shed or huddle against his mother's warmth, he can freeze to death in a short time.

4

Several years ago during one spring storm, several heifers, drifting in front of the wind, lost their calves. Bernard Betz, my cousin, spent a good part of the day bringing the calves into the bunkhouse, where they dried off under a propane heater. When the storm ended, the calves were reunited with their mothers.

Many calves are born out in the hills, away from the warm sheds and the barns. These calves depend on the mother cows' survival skills to find deep, sheltered draws or tree-lined hillsides until the storm passes.

Back in the house, I throw another log on the fire in the fireplace and wait for my husband Rich to get home from his job in Sheridan, forty miles away. The road between here and there is often bad during snowstorms, but Rich has the four-wheel-drive pickup, so he should have no trouble getting home.

By morning, the storm has blown itself out. The fire, banked last night, has burned down to coals, so I find some kindling to restart it. Outside, the new snow lies in wavy drifts on the alfalfa field. The sun, just up, is slanting its cold rays across the snow, making the drifts a silvery color, and making the snow-covered trees sparkle. It looks like a white fairyland.

In comparison to last night's wintery wind and cold, the day is still and mild. It still smells faintly like spring as I feed my cows and open the gate so they can scrounge through the snow for winter-dry grass. Then I jump into the pickup and drive the four miles out to Dad's house to get ready for a day of feeding.

CALVING

When cows were cheap and plentiful, ranchers didn't worry too much about calving losses. A few were expected each year from storms, predators, and calving difficulties. Many ranchers had only a foggy idea of the number of cattle they had, and as many as they had, a few calves lost was nothing to get upset about.

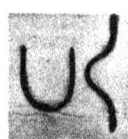 Today, each cow is worth several hundred dollars, many ranchers have smaller herds, and every calf counts. Ranchers with smaller herds can watch each cow and lose few calves.

Many times the first-calf heifers are bred to Longhorn or Mexican bulls to insure small, slim calves that will give the heifers little trouble. In registered herds and more and more in commercial herds, birth weights are recorded and kept, and operators can breed to bulls that sire calves with low birth weights.

This is easier on the cow and the rancher. A cow that has had trouble calving may develop scar tissue and be difficult to breed again. There is also the chance of losing both cow and calf in a long, futile labor.

A misty rain is falling today and will probably turn to snow tonight. No one is around the ranch buildings when I drive in, but I see the pickup in the horse pasture above the house. It is muddy in the pasturelands, so I hike up to see what is happening.

Dad is here, and Mom. Lying on the ground is Patches, Mom's Holstein-cross heifer that Mom hopes will make a milk cow. Patches is mooing softly in pain, trying to calve. Two of the calf's legs are protruding. One leg is broken, with blood running out over the pinkish hide.

"What happened?"

"Patches is having trouble, and your Dad can't pull the calf. We think she got bred to the neighbor's Charolais bull."

"Is the calf dead?" I don't like the broken leg, dangling limply.

"I'm sure it is. We've been trying to pull it for two hours. It's just too big."

"You'd better take her to the vet. He can Caesarean it."

"We can't get her to the chute to get her in the stock truck. She's about worn out."

"We'll have to take her in," Dad says. "I think we can tie her in the pickup bed. I don't think she'll try to jump out, she doesn't even want to get up." The pickup has no stock racks, and if the cow jumped out she could break her neck or leg on the pavement. The pickup is four-wheel drive, otherwise Dad couldn't have driven up here in the mud.

Between the three of us and the handyman jack attached to a rope around the cow's shoulders, we push and winch Patches into the pickup bed. She lies there, not trying to put up a fight. I wonder if she will even make it through this alive.

Dad drives the pickup slowly out the gate, slithering in the slick mud, and heads down the graveled road toward town. Patches still lies quietly in the back. Mom and I go in the house to wait until Dad comes back to tell us how the cow is.

Mom is upset, and so am I. We had hoped that Patches would be a good milk cow, producing enough milk to feed both us and her calf. Now, with the difficulty of the too-big calf and any post-calving complications, she may be ruined for life. Scar tissue may prevent her from having another calf, and no calf means that the cow will produce no milk.

Mom and I don't say much, and I put on some water for hot tea. It will taste good on a day like this, and will help us to relax.

"We should have taken her up right away," Mom says, "but she was pretty far along when we found her. I hope we didn't hurt her too much trying to pull the calf."

Two hours later, the pickup pulls into the driveway, and Dad comes in. "The vet says the cow will be okay, and that she should be able to have other calves. The calf is dead, but we already knew that."

"Well, at least the cow is fine, and we didn't lose her too," Mom says, relieved.

I pour Dad a cup of hot tea and we watch the rain outside. It's good to be in next to the fire.

The morning is clear; the snow never came last night. Instead, the cloud cover blew away, leaving the temperature standing at zero. Yesterday's muddy ground is frozen today as we drive out across it to feed.

There are lots of cattle on the feed ground today but only two calves. The other calves must be bedded down in the draws, out of the wind and cold. Up on the hillside there is a lone cow, and she makes no move to come in to get the feed.

8

"I'll bet she's got a calf up there," Dad says. "I don't know why else she would be up there alone." Cows normally like company, except when they go off alone to calve.

"I wonder if it's okay?" I ask. "I don't see it standing up."

"She probably has him layed down in a brush. After we feed, we'll go up and check her," Dad says, then adds, "If we drive up now, the whole bunch will follow us. Maybe just feed off half the hay, maybe some more will come in."

Dad does have a valid point about the cows following us. I climb up on the haystack in the pickup and begin to cut the strings.

I feed off fifteen bales, then pound on the cab of the pickup so Dad will stop and let me inside. There is no real road up to where the cow is, so we make one, bouncing across the sage and rough, frozen ground.

In front of the cow is a new calf, stretched out flat on the cold ground.

"Probably dead," Dad says. "It was too cold last night and he chilled down. Probably never even got up."

If a calf can't get on his feet right after birth and get dried off by his mother's tongue, he has little chance of survival in the cold.

Dad gives the cow a shovelful of cake and walks closer to the calf. He is alive, but just barely. The flat sides hardly move with his breathing. The cold air, the frozen ground, and the calf's wet hide have nearly killed him. He has given up on life. It is now up to us to get him interested in living.

Dad lifts the calf and tries to stand him on his feet, but his weak knees bend, refusing to hold him up. The cow moos worriedly as Dad half-lifts, half-drags the calf to the pickup and boosts him inside the cab, laying him near the heater vent. The calf is limp, not even struggling to get away. It is just too much trouble.

9

Dad arranges the calf so he can ride comfortably, while I cut the strings on a hay bale to feed some to the cow. She eats greedily, having already given the calf up for dead.

We bounce back across the sage and ditches to feed the rest of the hay. The pickup cab is suffocating, and I am glad to get back outside in the cold, nipping wind.

Many of the cattle are stringing in from across the hill and up the road. I can count fifty head. There should be sixty or so in this pasture, so we have most of them. It doesn't take long to feed the fifteen bales that we have left. Using the scoop shovel, I push off the cake, wondering where the cow is that usually follows right behind the pickup, eating right off the tailgate. She must be one of the missing cattle today.

Dad stops and I jump back into the cab, taking care not to hit the calf lying at my feet. Even though my fingers and face are numb from the cold, the cab feels stifling. I shed my heavy hat and coat, forgetting that I have to shut the gate on the way out.

"We'll feed him before we go feed again," Dad says, stopping for the gate. I jump out quickly to shut it, getting chilled in my light shirt. Getting back in, I pet the calf, who is shivering violently now. I hope he will live after we get the warm milk in him.

When we get back to the house, Dad carries the calf down to the barn, calling back to me to put a little brandy in the calf's milk. While he is fixing the calf a bed of straw under a heat lamp, I heat some milk and look around for a pop bottle to put it in. Calves that are starved or ill seem to forget how to nurse, and the only way to save their lives is to force-feed them by pouring the milk down their throats.

Failing to find a pop bottle, I settle for a huge whiskey bottle as the next best thing. The bottle has a pump fixture on top, but with the pump taken off, the bottle has a narrow enough neck for our purpose. The milk is hot by the time I

10

get back to the kitchen. I pour it into the bottle and dig into the refrigerator to find the brandy. I pour a little bit into the milk. It will give the calf a quick warm-up.

When I get back to the barn, the calf is lying stretched out under the heat lamp on a soft, deep bed of straw.

"This is the only bottle I could find. It should work."

Dad pours some milk into the calf's mouth, and I can see the throat muscles contract to swallow it. At least he can still eat, but he makes no effort to nurse when Dad sticks his fingers into the calf's mouth.

"Well, we'll leave him here and finish our feeding, then we'll feed him again," Dad says. I feel the calf's body to make sure that the heat lamp, suspended from the ceiling, won't make the calf too hot while we are gone. The red body is warm, but not hot.

We take the bottle back into the house, and Dad puts the last of the brandy to a more enjoyable purpose, warming his blood instead of the calf's. We have two more herds of cattle to feed, then we will be done for the day.

By morning, the wind has died down and the sun is shining, warming the chill air. It will be a nice day. The calf is still lying under the heat lamp, but he can nurse off a bottle now, and he takes the milk with enthusiasm. Dad stands him up, and he can stand, but shakily.

"Let's take him back out and see if the old cow remembers him. If she will take him, I think he'll make it."

If the cow doesn't take him, he'll be a bum, and one of us will have to feed him on a nipple bucket or a calf nursing bottle until he is old enough to wean.

"Do you think she will take him?" I ask more for conversation than any other reason.

"I guess we'll find out," Dad says.

Mom is helping today, and she agrees.

11

The cow is where we left her yesterday. Sometimes the cow will go back several times to a dead calf, not quite understanding why the calf won't get up.

"There she is." I point to her.

"Is that the same one?" Mom asks.

"Yeah, that's her," Dad says. "Let's see if she'll remember him." We bounce across the sagebrush again, only this time the calf tries to stand up on the floor of the cab. Mom holds him to keep him from getting hurt.

Dad stops, and Mom and I get out. Dad lifts the calf out and sets him down by his mama. I jump into the back to give the cow a scoop of cake.

"Here's your calf, cow," Dad tells her.

The cow never expected to see her calf again. I'm sure that she had given him up for dead. She can't believe that this is her calf, alive and well. She sniffs him, mooing a little in wonder. Then she licks him eagerly, almost upsetting his shaky stance. The calf, knowing instinctively where the food is, tries to find the bag to nurse, but the excited cow keeps turning to lick the calf to convince herself that it is hers. I can almost hear her excited questions. "Where were you? I thought you were gone for sure. What happened? Are you alright?" Despite the cow's excitement, the calf finds the teat and begins to nurse. The cow stands quietly now, convinced that the calf is hers, and lets him nurse.

Even though today promises to be warm, the nights are still chilly. If the calf gets chilled again, he could catch pneumonia and die. We leave him to his meal while we feed the other cattle. Then Dad boosts him into the pickup bed so we can take him back home. Mom rides in the back with the calf to keep him from falling out, and I drive the pickup off slowly while Dad brings up the rear, driving the cow along behind.

12

The cow must have once been a bum calf; she is much gentler than the average range cow. She follows behind the pickup, sticking her big head inside the bed to take the pieces of cake out of Mom's hand. Watching her in the rearview mirror, I know that she is the one that was missing yesterday, the one that eats cake right off the tailgate.

I drive very slowly, the pickup in low gear. The cow seems more interested in the cake than in her calf, but as long as she is following, we don't care why. It takes almost three times as long as usual to cover the mile and a half back to the house. Once there, we put the cow and calf in the barn, where the calf will be warm and out of the wind.

It feels good to know that the calf will live and that we were instrumental in saving the little, newborn life. If the cow had birthed the calf back in the hills, away from the feed ground, the story would have been very different.

When we drive up into the meadow to feed, we notice a cow with a swollen udder. We suspect that she has lost her calf, probably on the same night that the one we just saved was born. It is no use to look for the calf; the sagebrush flats are ideal hiding places, and even a live calf is hard to find. All we can do is feed the cows and go on to the next pasture.

In the morning there is a hint of snow on the wind. We feed the cows, then drive across the ridges to make sure that everything is okay and to check for sick cows or calves. We were over there just three days ago, and everything looked healthy.

Today we find a bunch of cows, about fifteen or so, and feed them the hay we saved and some cake. Bandit, a cow of mine named for her brown eyepatches, looks bagged up, her udder very swollen. We saw her calf three days ago and ear-marked it so we could be sure to find it at branding. It was young, but it looked healthy then.

13

"The calf is probably too young to take it all," Dad tells me. Often a cow with a very young calf will produce too much milk for it. As the calf grows older, he can take more.

"Maybe we had better check it, though. It may not be getting enough to eat."

Dad parks the pickup and we walk up the trail that Bandit had come down.

Bandit sees us heading in that direction, and she trots before us, leading us to where she left the calf. The calf is there, dead. Poor Bandit. She seems to think that we have come to help her. She leads us right up to the poor little dead calf, sniffs it, then looks up at us as if to say, "Here he is, please get him up." She looks at us, then back at the calf. Dad feels it, and it is cold and stiff. Obviously it has been dead for quite a while.

"Damn," Dad says. "She starved it to death. Dumb cow."

"It looked fine the other day," I say. "It looked good."

Dad is blaming himself for the calf's death. "We should have taken her in and milked her out. But I thought he was getting enough." We both feel bad about the calf's death. It is possible that we could have prevented it, and that makes it even harder to take.

"We didn't know. He seemed fine when we saw him." I am trying to make Dad feel better, but I don't think I'm doing a very good job.

"Well, nothing we can do now. We should sell her anyway. She's getting old."

She was. She had been born during a spring blizzard in 1974 that froze the tips of her ears off. That made her eight years old, and her udder was half-spoiled.

"Yeah," I said. "She wants us to help her. Sorry, old girl. We can't help it now. It's too late."

14

We leave Bandit standing over the still, dead body of the calf. She seems to be hoping that we have worked a miracle and brought her calf back to life.

After lunch, Mom and I ride out on horseback to bring in another cow whose bag is swollen because the calf is too young to take all the milk. If the cow is left too long in this condition, her udder will be damaged as Bandit's was. This cow is young, and we want to keep her healthy for several more years.

It is a chilly afternoon, so we bundle up in down coats, and I zip into my chaps. The horses are frisky, and Gazelle tries to buck, shaking his head and dancing under me. I let him run for a while, getting the winter cold out of his muscles.

Finally, I pull him up for a moment, enjoying the panorama below me. I can see for miles down the valley. I see the trees along Clear Creek and the Big Horn Mountains in the distance. A white veil moves across the lowlands, a curtain of snow coming at us. It swirls around us, a ghost's wedding veil, spinning as she rushes past, and rushes away down the valley and across the hills. One tiny squall, no more.

The cows are just below us, and they run for their calves as we ride up. The cow and calf we want head in the right direction, the calf looking like a kid in a costume, with his black body and white face masked in black.

The wind is cold, and by the time we get the cow and calf to the home pasture, the sun is behind the mountains and it is getting dark. We push the cow and calf faster and corral them. Tomorrow morning Dad will put the cow in the squeeze chute and milk out the too-big bag until the calf can take all the milk.

The house is light and warm when we come in, leaving the cold, dark night shut out.

"We got 'em," I tell Dad, who is reading the paper.

"Good job," he says.

15

TRAIL DRIVE

The words trail drive evoke romantic pictures in the minds of many. People imagine longhorned steers winding their way to the markets of Kansas and the East, pushed along by tough, sinewy cowboys on half-broke horses.

Trail drives today are not quite the same. Long-horns, at least in those great numbers, are a thing of history. Today a trail drive more often consists of white-faced Herefords or red and black Angus.

The distances are not as great, either; drives seldom cover more than a hundred miles. Many Wyoming ranchers lease land in the Big Horn Mountains, trailing the cattle up in the spring and back to the lowlands for the winter.

And cowhands seldom sleep under the stars anymore; often they are accompanied by a camper trailer for the night, or, if the cattle are behind a fence, the hands go home for the night.

The drive you are about to join is a drive we made for several years from our Buffalo land to the ranch near Clearmont.

The day of the drive starts early. My phone rings at 3 A.M.

"Yeah, I'm up," I mutter sleepily into the receiver. I know it's Dad, calling to see if I'm awake at this hour.

"Cynthia, are you coming out for breakfast?" Dad asks.

"On my way. How's the weather?"

"Chilly. Dress warm."

"Figures. See you later."

I leave Richard asleep. He'll go to work later in Sheridan as a taxidermist.

The driveway is black in the early morning, but up above the stars are coldly brilliant. The pickup grinds once, then starts. The April morning air is cold, making me shiver even through my layers of clothing.

During my four-mile trip, the pickup headlights cut a swath through the sable darkness. Dad's house lies in darkness, except for one lighted window.

I smell breakfast as I come in. Floury biscuits and the hickory-smoke smell of bacon frying. The house is warm and light after the cold, dark morning.

Mom nods a greeting from the stove.

"Looks like a clear day," I remark.

"Looks like it," Dad says, sipping on a before-breakfast cup of tea. "Want a cup of tea?"

"I'll get it." I pour the hot water from a kettle heating on the potbellied coal stove in the corner that provides heat for the kitchen.

Linda Sue, my sister, comes sleepily out of her bedroom, her blond hair rumpled. She's five years my junior, back home today for the trail drive.

"You gonna ride today?" I tease her a little. She's not a horsewoman.

She yawns at me, then grins. "Nope. I get to ride in the

nice, warm pickup and drink Pepsi all day." Linda Sue drives the flag pickup, the vehicle that goes ahead of the cattle to warn other vehicles of their approach.

"Lazy," I grin back. Then I turn to Dad and ask if the horse herd is corraled. The horses run in a large pasture, and we bring them in to a smaller corral when we need them.

"Yep. They're in."

After breakfast, Mom, Dad, Linda, and I shrug into heavy goosedown coats and put overshoes on over our boots for extra warmth. At this time of year and this early in the day we never know if it will be cold or warm later.

The horses are jumpy in the cold and dark. They pretend not to recognize our bulky, dark shapes and blow frosty air out of their nostrils in snorty "Whuffs."

They feel frisky in the cold, and it takes a while to catch the three we need for the day's riding. We saddle them by the pale, white light of the yard light, then lead them up the chute and into the stock truck.

When we arrive at the Buffalo ranch, the sky is a pale orange color in the east, a preview of the coming day. A pheasant chuckles near the creek, and somewhere an owl hoots lonesomely.

Unloading at the corrals, each rider checks bits, reins, and cinches, left loose for the horse's comfort during the long ride.

Ready to go, I swing aboard my little Arabian, Gazelle. He's seventeen years old this year and still going strong. He jerks his finely made head and tries to buck, excited by the new country and stimulated by the cold. I pat his arched neck, which is covered with a long, thick mane.

"I know. You think you're pretty mean." Gazelle nods his head and bucks playfully again. He would be as surprised as I if he ever succeeded in dumping me during these early morning sessions. We both enjoy them.

18

Bernard Betz, my cousin and a partner in the ranch, and his wife Linda are already mounted, gathering up the winter-wild yearlings for the long, thirty-mile trip back to Clearmont. I jig Gazelle over to help them. The cattle take it into their heads to run, and they stream down the bank of Clear Creek.

Clear Creek starts high in the Big Horn Mountains and runs through Buffalo and this ranch. Farther down the valley, it also runs past my house near Clearmont before it flows into the Powder River. This time of the year it is still iced over, but in places the swift moving water is free of ice, and the yearlings can drown if they fall in.

Gazelle and I gallop over to head them, leaping the narrow irrigation ditches that run through this hayfield. Surrounded by the riders, the yearlings grudgingly turn and run back toward the gate. Dad, waiting nearby, opens it and rides out on the shaled road to turn them in the right direction. Still running, the yearlings miss the gate and run up the fence.

Bernard rushes past me, turning on his store of language picked up in the army and throughout his years on ranches. The cattle ignore the language but stop and mill around when confronted by the horses. Finally, one sees the opening, and they escape out of it, heading down the red shale road toward the highway and the road home.

The road is fenced with barbed wire on both sides, and there is little the cattle can do to escape. They walk along, some panting a little from their wild dash.

A small rodent joins the cattle, trying to cross the road. He runs a short distance and is confronted by a cow's hoof. Turning, he finds himself facing another hoof. He is in danger of being trampled by the huge animals, but he finds an opening and darts back into the winter-dead weeds along the road's edge.

19

The riders joke about it, commenting on weight and prices per pound of the rodent. It is decided that he wouldn't bring much on the market.

The iron bridge that spans Clear Creek looms ahead, the trusses guarding the sides and spanning the bridge overhead. The cattle, frightened, balk at this monster. They turn and run back, the leaders shouldering their way back into the herd, and the tail-enders turning and running back to get away. The riders whirl their experienced cow horses, keeping the horses between the cattle and their freedom. The cattle mill, refusing to go across the bridge. Several crowd against the wire fence where it joins the bridge, pushing the wires and straining them.

"Hold back," Dad says. "Don't push them through the fence."

I circle Gazelle back, and Mom moves her horse out of the way, giving the yearlings a little slack. For a long moment it is a stalemate. The cattle stand with their heads down, staring at the bridge in wonder. Their breath rises above them in vapors in the gray dawn air. Then one puts a tentative foot on the planking, testing it, bugging out his eyes and bowing his short neck. He tries another foot and is crowded onto the bridge by the crunch of yearlings moving behind him. Another tries the bridge, and they begin to move across. The riders breathe a sigh of relief—last year they broke through the fence—and slowly push them across.

Their feet make a hollow rumble on the planking and they begin to run, frightened by the sound and by the sight of the water and ice beneath them. The riders on Highway 16 spread out. Dean Floate, an old friend who will drive Bernard's pickup and horse trailer along, is mounted for the moment to help us cross the pavement. Linda Betz has ridden through the herd to help on the other side. Between them, Dean and Linda form an alley for the cattle. They also hold

20

up any early morning traffic traveling the secondary pavement between Buffalo and Clearmont.

The lead cattle pause to sniff the frosty, unfamiliar surface. Then they trot across, eyes on the stretch of open grasslands on the other side. Once there, the yearlings begin to run again, and Linda Betz leaps her big bay horse out to head them, or at least keep them going in the right direction. Bernard and Charlie Holland, the neighbor whose land we are crossing, gallop up to help her.

Charlie Holland will show us the shortest, best route to take across his land, and his wife will meet him with their pickup truck and horse trailer at the county road about eight miles away.

Mom, Dad, and I bring up the drag, or end of the herd. There are, in every herd, ambitious cattle and lazy ones. The ambitious ones stay in the lead, trotting most of the way. The lazy ones make up the drag. Bernard, Charlie, and Linda will hold up the lead of the herd at a gate just up the pasture a ways to wait for the drag to catch up.

If the herd isn't kept at least somewhat together, the lead gets too far ahead, and the riders are too scattered to be of much use if a stampede occurs. If the herd gets too spread out, cattle in between the lead and the drag can slip away down a draw or across a hill and be lost.

When the herd is gathered together again, we push them through the gate and turn them east, into the rising sun, up a red shale hill. The top is lined with lumpy red rocks left over from some long ago volcano.

The rays of the rising sun touch the snow on the tops of the Big Horn Mountains to the west, turning it to silver and the mountains to a deep sky blue. The rays slant across the land, making long silver-gold fingers in the valleys. The land under the cattle's feet is a mixture of fall grasses, golden-brown, and spring snow. The sun gives the whole landscape a pinkish hue, tinged with gold.

21

The cattle stretch before us like a snake, twisting and turning around rocks and washed-out holes. They move at a walk, sometimes at a trot. We ride beside and behind them to keep them moving and pointed in the right direction.

Bernard is the point man, riding in the lead, opening gates and giving the cattle a leader to follow. Linda Betz and Charlie Holland ride swing, near the front of the herd on either side, to direct them. Dad and I ride between the flank, near the back, and the drag, where Mom rides to keep them pushed up.

We push the cattle to the top amid the red chunks of lava rock and head them out across the long expanse of grassland stretching across the hilltops. The valley stretches out below us, and hills and foothills climb up to the majestic Big Horn Mountains. The town of Buffalo, four miles behind us, sends white smoke up into the cold air. Cars on Interstate 90 rush past, people on their way. I feel an urge to be there, driving, but it passes, leaving me glad that I'm on my horse behind the cattle.

The sun climbs higher in the sky, turning the cold morning air warmer. The yearlings move at a walk now. We are leaving the snow country, and the hillsides are bare. Ahead are many more hills to climb or go around, using old deer and cattle trails left from other drives. The hillsides are rocky, and I worry about Gazelle's unshod feet. We take the hills carefully, skirting the big rock piles and trying to find sandy soil. It is easy for a rock to lodge itself in the soft sole of a horse's foot and lame him, much like a rock in a human's shoe.

The cattle wind in and out of the hills like a red and white Hereford ribbon, varied with patches of black Angus and yellow Charolais crosses. The sun, shining off their winter coats, gives the whole herd a velvety effect.

22

By nine we come to an open water hole, pocketed in the hills. The cattle see it from the hilltop and rush down, kicking up red shale dust and half-obscuring the leaders from our sight in the red mist. The dust floats back gently, tasting gritty in my mouth and stinging as a piece buries itself in my eye.

The herd reaches the water hole, and the cattle pile up to drink, thirsty from the drive. Several of the riders dismount and tie heavy coats to the backs of their saddles with saddle strings, leather strips built into the saddles from early days for that purpose. I still feel comfortable, so I leave my jacket on for the time being.

After the cattle get their drink, the horses get their chance to sample the now muddy water. Gazelle snorts at it but wades out in the mud to drink, knowing that it may be a long ways to the next water stop.

Ahead is a long grade, and the yearlings move sluggishly toward it, then balk at the thought of climbing it. Some start up, then halfway up turn to head back down the hill. The riders crowd them before their rebellion can spread to the rest of the herd. They turn, only to dive off the road's shoulder and run back toward the pond. I rein Gazelle around to head after them, hoping there are no holes to throw me and my horse.

Galloping up at an angle to the cattle is Bernard, colorfully telling them just what he thinks of their outburst. Between the two of us, the cattle turn back up the hill.

Topping the ridge, we can see the pavement of the county road below, about four miles away. Starting from Buffalo and dwindling off into the distance on its way to Arvada, Wyoming, some fifty miles away, the road is called Crazy Woman Creek road, as much of it runs along Crazy Woman Creek.

By ten fifteen we come to the pavement.

23

No reason to fear trouble here, as the pavement is fenced with barbed wire on both sides. Gazelle's free, fast walk is too fast now, and given a chance he would walk right through the slower-moving herd of cattle. I dismount, loosen his cinch, and lead him, stretching saddle-cramped legs. Gazelle walks along at my shoulder, glad to be rid of my weight on his back.

Ahead I see the lead pickup, with Linda Sue driving. She took Interstate 90 from Buffalo and the exit for this road to meet us here. Now she will go ahead of the herd, stopping on top of hills and around curves to warn other drivers that the herd of cattle is moving along the road. Dean, with the pickup and horse trailer, falls in behind the herd, doing the same thing.

We meet one car, a rancher's pickup. He knows cattle and drives through the herd slowly, waving at the riders with the herd. He's a friend of Dad's, so they stop and chat a minute before he moves on.

The birds haven't come back from the southlands yet, but the nonmigrating birds twitter as they fly past. A black and white magpie, sleek and shiny, lands on a fence post and studies us, head cocked.

By noon we come to the fence line and auto gate that divides the paved road from the graveled road, and one ranch from another. The land on the other side of the gate is no longer fenced, but open grasslands, stretching as far as we can see. We push the cattle through the gate after Bernard opens it and let them spread out over the grass to eat or sleep until the lunch break is over.

The pickup truck is waiting on the other side of the gate with coolers of food and drinks, prepared and loaded up last night. The horses are tied to the trailer or hobbled, and fed a small feed of oats. Then we unload the coolers for our lunch.

There is bread, thick, homemade slices baked by Mom or Linda Betz, lunch meat, and potato salad. Beer, water, and pop make up the liquid refreshments. For dessert a spice cake, again homemade, looks delicious.

It has been a long time since breakfast, and a lot of work has gone into the morning hours. The cattle, too, are hungry, and they spread out to graze on the short, dry grass. Some are lying down, contently chewing cuds and soaking up the warm spring sunlight. It is warm for April, with the temperature up around sixty degrees. A light breeze has followed us from Buffalo and plays across the range, just enough to keep the spring coolness in the air.

Sitting in the shade of the pickup, Mom passes out suntan lotion, and I rub some on my face, which is already starting to burn a little. Linda Betz mentions that she meant to bring some today but forgot it.

The warm sun combined with a full stomach makes me sleepy, but I stretch the stiffness out of my arms and legs and get ready for the next part of the drive. The lunch break is over. Time to tighten cinches and move the cattle out.

The yearlings are scattered around the range, some in the cuts and draws looking for water, many on the flats eating grass. The riders split up, two riders taking the left side of the road and three taking the right. Cattle stare at us belligerently as we surprise them from their naps. One bunch, tired and mad, moves a little ways, and then two or three lie down, daring me to move them. I gallop over, and they resentfully get up again and move. Thinking they will go, I wheel around to head the bunch Bernard is chasing that wants to go back to Buffalo. While I am busy there, the other five I roused are stopped, watching their wild companions with interest. Seeing an opportunity for rest, the big rednecked one lies down again.

25

Cussing to myself, I head Bernard's bunch back to the road, then circle back to push up the lazy ones. Reluctance showing in their brown eyes, they heave themselves to their feet and go, finally, in the direction that I want them to go. I push them down into a draw, then up the other side to the road. Underneath the road is a five-foot-high cement culvert, put in by Johnson County to keep the spring floodwaters from rushing over the road and washing it out. I hear a splashing noise from inside this culvert. Curious, I circle Gazelle back around and lean down on his neck to look inside.

A white-faced yearling stares back at me, head down, water dripping from his muzzle. He looks surprised to see me and slowly backs out of the culvert, watching me warily all the time. Once out, he runs, bucking a little, to join the rest of the herd, which is moving down the road in front of Mom.

The other riders join us, bringing herds of 50, 60, and 75 yearlings. Altogether we should have 363. Strung out along the road it looks like 500 or more.

Dad rides up beside me. "Think we got 'em all?"

"I hope so. We combed the country pretty good back there. They should all be here."

The day is getting hotter. The breeze that followed us from Buffalo has died down, killed by the sun. I scan the sky eagerly for a cloud, but the sapphire sky is cloudless; the sun, even this early in the year, is dazzling, almost molten looking with heat.

The yearlings move slowly now, wanting to rest road-weary feet and legs. We push them relentlessly, anxious to get them bedded down and get the day over with. The drag plods slowly, immune now to the shouts and yells. At first they scared easily, but now they are tired and used to the riders behind them. Yelling only makes me hoarse, so I quit doing it and push the cattle along by hitting them with the ends of my bridle reins. This, too, loses its effect shortly. Gazelle,

26

tired also, reaches over and nips one with his big teeth. The yearling jumps a little, then settles down again into tired lethargy.

Gazelle sneezes, and the unexpected sound causes the yearlings to jump and trot a little ways before plodding along again. The leaders, stronger and wilder, are way ahead, walking fast. There is a gap between the leaders and the drag that could be filled by two cars. "Push 'em up," Dad says.

"I've been trying to. They don't move. Maybe Bernard will hold them up at the gate."

"Yeah, he wants to get a count on them. He thinks some may be missing."

"I hope not."

Something spooks the leaders, and Linda Betz and Mom rush to head the runaway. Bernard, on point, holds up his horse to see if they can get the wild ones back to the bunch. The cattle run up a hillside, then, as the riders turn them, bend back down to the road. The lead is now at the gate that separates one ranch from another. Stopped by the fence, the leaders spread out, grazing, within the circle made by the fence and riders, and wait for the drag to catch up.

Last year we used this area for a bedground for the cattle and put the horses in an empty hay corral overnight. Bernard and Linda brought their camper and slept in it here to be sure that they would be around when the cattle began to move in the early morning. There were wild turkeys gobbling in the trees just before dawn the next morning when we went to catch our horses. This year we will take the cattle farther, to a neighbor's ranch, where he has a small fenced pasture and a corral for our horses. It's still about four miles ahead.

The drag finally catches up, and Bernard opens the gate. "Push them slow. I'll get a count." I nod and hold Gazelle back, letting the cattle move through at their own pace. Bernard watches them intently, trying not to miss any. They trail through and keep going down the road.

"How's the count?" I ask.

"We're about six short. Must have missed them on the lunch stop. Cynthia, you and I'll go back and check the cuts back there. Some could be holed up."

I know what he means. The cattle, thirsty, looking for water, may have strayed farther than we thought. I hope we can find them without riding too far.

We ride back to where Dean has stopped the pickup, and the horses jump willingly into the stock trailer, glad to let it do their legwork. The pickup seat feels soft and comfortable after the hard saddle.

"If we find them, we'll put them in Christian's corral overnight, and Wallace can bring my stock truck back to pick them up in the morning," Bernard tells me.

I remember the corral, a well-made board structure near where we ate our lunch.

"Okay."

It doesn't take long to find the strays. They are lying in the shade of a tall, steep bank, full of grass and water from a spring nearby. They drive easily and give no trouble going into the corral. Bernard locks the gate, and we ride around the corral to make sure there is no other opening.

We load back up in the trailer and head back to the rest of the herd. At the herd, I unload near the drag, and Bernard goes on up to the point. We are almost to the bedground now, a welcome sight after this long day.

The shadows begin to lengthen, and the sun casts golden rays across the golden-brown pasture lands. The hills look soft and blurred, and the dust stirred up by the cattle covers everything with a fine film. The yearlings are tired, some panting with weariness. We are almost done; only two miles left, then we can feed the cattle a load of hay, unsaddle the horses, and go home to supper and bed.

28

The second day of the drive starts a little later, at 4 A.M. instead of 3. We don't have as far to drive to reach the cattle, and we don't have to trail them as far.

This morning is even colder than yesterday, and the stars are covered by clouds. The wind is blowing across the hills, biting through down coats and winter hats.

The sky is lighter in the east when we arrive at the bedground, but there will be no sun for a while.

"We may get caught in a storm," Dad says, his eyes on the clouds.

"The radio weather report didn't forcast one for today," Mom answers.

"We're guaranteed to get one," I comment, knowing Wyoming weather doesn't always conform with the weather reports.

The horses, knowing they are going to be ridden, run to the far side of the corral, snorting frost. "Oh, quit," I tell Gazelle affectionately. He bobs his head and stands waiting, lowering his head for the bridle and taking the bit in his soft mouth.

We saddle, mount up, and ride to the bedground, where the yearlings are already awake and looking for a way out of the pasture. One tries to cross the shallow creek, but Bernard is already there to head him off. Linda Betz and her daughter, Sheila, are rounding up yearlings on the far side of the pasture. I am surprised to see Sheila. She was down with the flu yesterday and didn't help. She must be feeling better today. Seeing Bernard's pickup and horse trailer parked near the road, empty, I gather that Dean is not here today.

Bernard turns to chase another runaway, and Gazelle and I splash out into the creek to turn back two more that would like to cross. The yearlings turn and run toward the rest of the herd, converging as the riders bring them in from different directions.

Once we get the herd together, we push up a hill to the open gate on top that takes them to the road. The yearlings refuse to see the opening and skid down the steep bank to get away. Linda and Sheila are there to head them. They turn and rush at us, trying to get back to the creek. The horses whirl and turn to stay in front of them. Finally, they turn back up the hill but mill around at the gate. A black one sees the opening and jumps through as if stung. The others follow. Bernard, on the road, blocks them from heading back to Buffalo. Linda Sue moves the pickup slowly down the road ahead of them. We are on the trail for another day.

Once the cattle are moving well in the right direction, Bernard rides up beside me. "Wallace and I are going back to get those yearlings we corraled yesterday. You guys take them to the next fence and hold them until we get back."

"Okay." That will leave Mom, Linda, Sheila, and me to keep the 350 yearlings moving along in the right direction.

The yearlings, rested, move faster than they did yesterday, sensing the coming storm and excited by the rising wind around us. Linda Betz is riding beside me, and I notice her sunburned nose from yesterday.

"Did you bring your suntan lotion today?" I laugh. The sun is nowhere in sight.

Linda grins. "I did. It's in my coat pocket."

She bounds off up the road bank to chase a stray.

The road twists and bends, and it seems like a long ways to the gate. The cattle refuse to stop when they come to the wire barrier; they run up the fence as it turns up the hillside. I gallop up to turn them, and they run back and break past Sheila. Mom and Linda rush to head them, and they crowd against the lower fence, threatening wires and unstable posts. The cattle are nervous, edgy with the wind and storm. They want to keep moving. It may be a long time before the men get back.

30

"We'd better take them along," I yell over the wind. "I don't know when the men will be back. We may lose them."

"I think so," Mom yells back.

I ride up to Linda. "Shall we move them out? They're apt to go through the fence."

"I know. I think we can take them along. I'll get the gate." Linda rides through the herd slowly, not wanting to spook them into a run. Mom, Sheila, and I watch, alert for trouble, but the cattle stand, waiting.

They crowd through the gate, eager to be off. The cold begins to bite through my coat, and my fingers, in cotton gloves, are getting cold. The wind begins to bring tiny drops of sleet. "We're gonna get stormed on," I yell at Mom. She nods, busy with the cattle.

The cattle go along at a trot and cover ground quickly. We trot to keep up and gallop when they veer off the road. I feel like a rustler in the Old West, moving the herd fast to stay ahead of the law and the storm.

Riding into the storm, the sleet hits my face like tiny needles, stinging yesterday's sunburn. I turn my head sideways to ride into it. The storm is gaining force, the wind is harder, and the sleet is turning to snow. Huge flakes are blotting out the landscape.

Ahead of us is a long, steep grade, turning off this road at a ninety degree angle. We have to push the cattle up this grade. A difficult job anytime, as cattle do not like to go up hills; they prefer to go around them or wind up them slowly. It will be even harder to take them up in the face of the storm.

I gallop ahead to turn them up the hill, and the herd splits, half going calmly in the right direction and half running to the left across a flat riddled with prairie dog holes, which can throw a horse and break his leg. The yearlings seem oblivious to the holes in their stampede across the flat.

31

Mom, Linda, and Sheila gallop after them, taking it a little cautiously but getting the herd turned toward the hill.
The yearlings refuse to take the trail that leads to the road
I'm on. The riders and cattle look small below me as I push
my herd farther on the road, higher as we climb up the
grade.

There is little I can do to help the riders below. I have to
keep my herd moving and keep the cattle from going off the
road to the right, where they can lose themselves in a deep,
rough draw. The snow and the intervening hills block my
view of the herd below me. My herd moves peacefully.

It's eerie up here, all by myself in the storm. It's as
though my horse, the small herd of cattle, and I are in a
world of our own, a cold world of snow and wind that cuts
us off from the rest of the world. I think of the song "Ghost
Riders in the Sky," and almost expect to see them ride out of
the gray sky with their ghostly herd.

The ghostly herd does not materialize, but a white-faced
yearling comes over the ridge behind me, followed by others.
Mom, Linda, and Sheila have gotten the herd to the top. I
don't see any riders, but they will be along.

Over the wind I hear the motor of a vehicle and turn my
horse to see the stock truck, followed by Bernard's pickup
and horse trailer. Dynamite, Dad's horse, whinnies from the
trailer, and Gazelle answers.

Dad stops for a moment, so I ride over to talk. "Getting
them, I see," Dad says.

"Mom, Linda, and Sheila are bringing some up from
below. They split up."

"I'd better get. That road may be slick up ahead."

The road ahead is not graveled but hard-packed clay
that gets muddy and slippery when wet. The natives call it
gumbo.

Bernard waves as he moves slowly through the herd behind the truck. They are soon swallowed up by the storm.

32

The wind is stronger here on the ridge, and the storm is blowing directly at us, coming off the Big Horn Mountains to the northwest. The cattle, not liking the push into the storm, break off suddenly and run to the left, heading for a draw and shelter from the storm. I turn to head them, but I can make out Bernard's outline in the storm. He must have unloaded from the trailer and come back to help. To my left I hear the hoofbeats of a galloping horse, and Linda Betz comes through the storm and runs to help Bernard.

If the cattle get away now and shelter up in the deep, rough draws, it could take several hours of hard riding in the blinding storm to find them and bring them back or sort them out of the neighbors' cattle. Keeping them bunched and moving into the storm is difficult. They want to turn tails to it and drift ahead of the wind. Mom appears beside me, and then Sheila, pushing up the last of the rebels.

"Where's the lead?" Mom asks.

"They broke away out there." I point into the snow swirls. "Bernard and Linda are after them. I thought I'd better keep these together."

The cattle move at a walk, heads down, as though pushing against a barrier. It is. A barrier of wind and snow. Gazelle walks with his head sideways to escape the stinging snow particles. His ears already wear a furry layer of snow. The snow stings my face as I gallop into it to turn the cattle. My face and hands begin to feel numb with cold.

It feels almost warm when I turn my back to the wind. My legs are white with a coating of snow, and body heat is beginning to melt it, making my thighs wet and cold.

The lead is somewhere, we can't see it in the storm. The best we can do is to push our own bunch toward the home pasture.

Suddenly, the herd is swallowed up by the rest of the cattle, coming in from the left, running away from the riders and the storm. Bernard and Linda got them turned! I gallop

33

up on the right of the herd as the cattle try to rush across the road and down into the draw on the other side. If they get down in the draw, turning them will be a long, hard job in the rough country.

The cattle see me and stop, startled, and it gives me the extra time I need to get them headed. Vanquished, they turn and docilely head back to the road. It isn't far to the gate now, and the home pasture. The trail drive will soon be over for another year.

SCATTERING BULLS

Before 1878, Wyoming cattle were mostly Texas
Longhorns, brought north to fatten on the rolling grasslands. The rancher paid little attention to what bulls
were used for breeding, and he knew nothing of pedi-
grees or registrations.

In 1878, Alexander Swan imported several Herefords from England to cross with the
range cattle and improve the breed. The
Herefords were stockier and put on
weight faster than the Longhorns. The
meat was also a great deal more palata-
ble, owing to the marbling in it.

Today, the Herefords, along with Red and Black
Angus, make up the bulk of Wyoming beef breeds.
With the cattle industry needing fast-growing, bigger
cattle that produce a good rate of gain in the feedlots, a
good bull is important to the cattle raiser. A bull can
sire thirty to fifty offspring a year, and his characteristics, good or bad, are passed along to a good percentage
of the herd.

Most breeders of registered bulls keep records of a
bull's birth weight, weaning weight, and rate of weight
gain so the buyer can know what to expect from most of
the bull's offspring.

It's warm today, even in the early morning. The sun is barely up, and everything looks green and gold because of the June grass and the sunlight.

Dad, Bernard, and I ride abreast, heading to the bull pasture. By scattering the bulls—putting them out with the cows to be bred—in June, we can expect a few March calves, although most will be born in April and May.

The bulls are restless, walking the fence and bellowing, knowing it is breeding season. I hate driving bulls, and I especially hate driving Herefords. Their long, curving horns look dangerous, and they can be. This time of year they are full of energy and orneriness, and there are several fights among the bulls.

The older bulls rule the herd, but the more aggressive young bulls won't give up, and they are beaten again and again. Still, the bulls seldom hurt each other. When the bull calves are weaned, lead weights are screwed into their horns, gradually pulling the horns down into the distinctive round moon shape that is a mark of the Hereford breed.

The bulls have wintered well on pasture, hay, and mineral tubs. There are eight Black Angus, brand new bulls bought in February. They are to be crossed with the Hereford cows to obtain the black-baldy, a black cow with a white face. These bring premium prices on the market now because of their high rate of weight gain in the feedlots. I can remember when the buyers used to dock us for them and didn't want anything but a straight-bred animal. Things change, and we have to be flexible.

Ten or twelve of the bulls are Herefords, to keep up a straight-bred Hereford herd. This black-baldy craze may be a fad, so we want to keep enough Herefords in case we have to switch back. Also, too many generations of crosses weakens the genetic structure of the herd, so we need the straight-bred cows to cross with the black bulls if the craze does last.

Three bulls are Mexican bulls, used to breed to the first-calf heifers. One of the Mexican bulls is wild-colored, which is a combination of black, white, and brown. Steers of this breed are often used in rodeos for roping stock, since their horns grow short and thick and are easily lassoed.

Today our job is to take several of the Hereford and Angus bulls to scatter. All the bulls are registered, to keep the quality of the herd high.

One of the Hereford bulls is limping. "Foot rot," Dad says, riding up beside the bull.

"We'd better take him in and give him some of those pills," Bernard says.

"I thought that mineral we got from Moorman feed was supposed to prevent that," I mention.

"Damn bulls won't eat it. Otherwise it probably would," Dad tells me.

"Oh." I ride off to push the other bulls up to the gate where Bernard is waiting to make sure they don't go past it and back into the pasture.

Four blacks and six Herefords make up our herd. They go out the gate and peacefully down the fence toward the corrals. Suddenly, a fight breaks out. Two Herefords on the outside edge of the herd are pushing heads, testing each other. They back apart, then one charges, pushing his opponent backwards, making him stagger on the rough ground. Another bull runs over to join in the action, bellowing deeply. I ride around them, watching for an opening so I can break up the fight and keep them moving. Some people use bullwhips to break up fights, but we don't have one.

The bulls struggle, each trying to push the other backwards. The younger bull is being pushed back farther and farther, and he finally breaks and runs—straight at me and Gazelle! Gazelle, wise to the ways of bulls, wheels and leaps

38

sideways, out of the way. A bull doesn't look where he's going when he is being chased, he just runs. To try to turn him could mean a bull, horse, and cowhand wreck.

The bull slows down, and I circle cautiously, heading him back to the herd. He goes reluctantly, but he goes, carefully skirting the other bull that just whipped him.

Dad, riding on the other side of the herd, is trying to break up a fight between a bull we are herding and one on the other side of the fence, in the pasture we just left. Dad doesn't want them to tear down the wire fence, and they can do a good job of it. I once had to fix a fence that two bulls had torn up. They loosened two posts, broke one, and ripped out so many staples that the four-foot fence was only half that high.

Dad tries to ride along the fence between the bulls, and one bull swings his head upward, his horn catching Lucy, Dad's horse, in the flank. The horn rips off a piece of skin about a foot long and an inch wide and flings it into the air.

Lucy, hurting and frightened, begins to buck, dropping her head between her forelegs and twisting, throwing her hind legs into the air. The bull, unsure what to do with the twisting, bucking horse beside him, gives up the fight and runs, bellowing his challenge.

Watching, there is nothing Bernard or I can do except hope that Dad can keep his seat and isn't thrown into the wire fence or under the bulls or the bucking horse. "Hang on!" I yell to Dad.

Dad fights for Lucy's weaving head, pulling on the reins. Finally, he gets her head pulled up and calms her down. My heart is pounding with heavy thuds. I ride up to see if Dad is okay, thankful that he wasn't thrown.

Dad is off, examining Lucy's flank. The skin is peeled off, exposing a streak of red muscle. The cut is not deep, mostly just a scrape, the kind a kid will get falling down on concrete. One or two drops of blood ooze out, but it is a

39

very minor cut. Lucy is trembling, and my own knees feel weak.

"Your horse okay?" Bernard asks.

"She'll be okay. As long as I don't kick her right there," Dad says. He pats Lucy's neck and swings back on her. Lucy jumps a little and is skittish, but the rodeo is over.

We regather the bulls, which have spread out across the field, and push them toward the corral. The bulls go peacefully, and the one with foot rot keeps up valiantly, holding his foot high to keep it off the rocks and clods.

When we get back to the corrals, Bernard goes to get the foot-rot pills, the antibiotic, and some medicine for Lucy's side. The bulls stand around the corral, switching tails and shifting feet. They are good-looking bulls, long, tall, and not too fat. Their backs are covered with tiny, bloodsucking flies.

Bernard comes back with the pills, medicine, and the spray rig, which is filled with insecticide. We will spray the bulls for flies before turning them out.

On foot now, Dad, Bernard, and I herd the bulls into the smaller corral where they can't get away from the spray mist. Bernard vaults over the fence and starts the gasoline motor that runs the rig, pumping spray out of the tank and into the hose. Dad climbs over the fence and takes the nozzel, turning the spray on the bulls.

The bulls mill around, bumping into each other as they try to get away from the spray and the noise of the motor. The spray soaks their backs and heads; it turns the brown hair of the Herefords darker and slicks down the straighter hair of the Angus. When the bulls are thoroughly soaked with spray, Bernard cuts the motor, and I open the gate to turn them out.

The insecticide smells moist and bitter. The flies, chased from the bulls and dying from the poison, find me and crawl up my arms and across my head. They hang dizzily or crawl

40

in staggering circles before falling off. I brush them off, but more come, tickling my bare arms and giving my flesh a crawly feeling.

The bull with foot rot is herded into the squeeze chute, where Dad catches the bull's head in the head catch. Then Dad pulls a rope that brings the sides together, to help hold the bull still. Dangling from the head gate with a rope is a pair of nose pliers, blunt-ended tongs that can be clamped to the bull's nose cartilage to pull the head around and hold it while Bernard administers the bolus (pill) with the help of a bolus gun.

The bull jumps and fights the chute, but he is held firm, and there is little he can do other than kick and jiggle his feet. The nose pliers and head squeeze hold his head fast. It doesn't take long to force the pills down his throat and give him the shot of antibiotic.

Bernard nods to Dad, and Dad loosens the pliers and chute, then the head gate, letting the bull out. The angry bull charges at Bernard, but Bernard scrambles up on the fence to safety. I worry about Dad, but he has already dived out the tiny gate by the front of the chute.

I have been on the fence all the time, not wanting to face an enraged bull weighing a ton or more. He glares evilly at us for a moment, his eyes red-rimmed. Then he shakes his head and paws the ground a little before walking off disdainfully.

"I'm glad you're going to be doctoring him and I'm not," I tell Bernard. An angry mother cow can tree me on a fence, and I am not about to face an angry bull if I can help it.

Bernard laughs.

We drive four of the bulls into the alleyway and up the chute to the stock truck. One bars the way into the truck and the others halt, uncertain what to do. No amount of yelling or beating on the bulls' thick hides with pieces of plastic pipe will move them past the guard. Finally, Bernard goes

41

around into the truck and catches the bull around the horns with a rope and ties him in the corner of the truck near the front, away from the tailgate. The other bulls now go peacefully up into the truck.

When Dad drops the endgate to lock them in, Bernard unties the guard. They are ready for the trip to the pasture. We will take these to the creek pasture and come back for our horses, as there is no room in the truck bed for them with the bulls. Bernard and Linda will drive the rest of the bulls to a pasture about a mile away.

"Do you think they will fight?" I ask Dad as I jump into the truck. Sometimes the bulls get into fights and tear up the stock racks and sideboards.

"I doubt it," Dad says, grinding the starter. It grinds once, then catches and takes off. As we pull out onto the county road, the truck wobbles and sways. The bulls are fighting.

"Hold on," Dad says. "I'll shake them up a little." Dad hits the brakes suddenly, causing the bulls to stagger to catch their footing and forget, for the moment, about hostilities.

The road is hard-packed and smooth, and we make good time.

Unloading a stock truck when there isn't a chute handy takes a little ingenuity. Dad finds a steep road bank that is about the same height as the bottom of the truck. He backs the truck up, and there is less than two inches between the bottom of the truck bed and the ground.

Dad pulls the rope attached to the pulley arrangement that opens the endgate. I shinny up the stock racks and yell to spook the bulls out of the truck. One bull tests the ground with his foot, then gingerly steps out. The rest follow.

Now we have to go back and get the horses, then we will be done for the day.

42

BRANDING

The practice of branding animals to prove ownership is very old, dating as far back as the time of the Egyptian pharaohs.

Branding came to the New World by way of the Spanish conquest of Mexico. From Mexico it spread north and was soon the established practice among 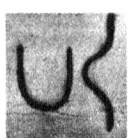 ranchers. A brand could not be erased, and it was an undisputed mark of ownership. Rustlers became adept at changing brands or branding over existing brands to cover up the theft. This worked well while the animal was alive, but if the animal was killed and skinned, the altered brand was plain.

Although the techniques of restraining the animal for branding have improved so much that two or three men can brand several hundred calves, the practice of using hot irons to apply the brand has not changed since early times.

Gazelle sidesteps restlessly. It's boring up here, just holding the herd while the men sort out the dry cows and the yearlings. "I know, boy. It won't be much longer." I pat his neck gently.

I know it can't be much longer. The sun has been down for two hours, and the last light has faded from the horizon. I look at my watch, turning the nonluminous dial to catch the inefficient starlight. "Ten-thirty," I mutter to my horse. It takes great concentration to make out the cattle shapes as I ride over to push them back into the herd. The moon has not yet risen, and the sky is black. The whole night curls around me like a black velvet blanket. The stars look like tiny static electrical sparks.

A nighthawk calls, his "preent" call soft and comforting in the dark night. One bird flies so close that his wings fan my face gently. I like the nighthawks. They are pretty gray birds, a cousin to the whippoorwills. In fact, a nighthawk's call can be interpreted as "Poor will, poor will."

A nighthawk eats great quantities of insects, and to watch one chase a miller moth or other insect is a study in speed, grace, and aerial ballet. The bird swoops and darts, following the insect's every move.

During the mating season, the nighthawks dive toward the earth at terrific speeds. As they bank and turn back upward in their flight, the air makes a deep, rough boom, like a mini-jet breaking the sound barrier.

Dad's voice, from the other side of the herd, startles me. "Move 'em out."

I can determine the other riders' locations from their voices, as "Okays" drift from all sides of the herd.

Soon the cattle are a slow-moving black mass.

We push them out a gate and turn them up the hillside

across a plowed wheatfield, fallow now, waiting for next spring when it will be seeded in wheat grass.

The field is rough and lumpy, except where the cattle have beaten a trail. We try to herd them down this trail, but several wild ones break away and run across the plowed field. I wheel Gazelle to go bring them back, and I can hear another rider also in pursuit.

"This is a good way to break your neck," I whisper to my horse. Almost on cue, Gazelle hits a clod and stumbles, throwing me up against the saddle horn. He catches his balance quickly, and I feel a cold wash of relief that he did not fall.

The cows are stubborn, but surrounded by three riders, they turn and go back to the herd.

The cattle trail through the gate into the pasture where they will be held overnight. "Eleven o'clock," Dad says, dismounting to shut the gate. I turn Gazelle's willing head homeward for supper and sleep.

Four A.M. comes too early. The buzzing alarm breaks my exhausted slumber. I struggle from the webs of dreams to shut it off, my head feeling too heavy to lift, and for a moment I fear that I can't lift it at all.

Breakfast is ready when I get to Dad's.

"You want coffee?" Mom asks when I walk in.

"You got any iced tea?" My mouth feels too dry to enjoy hot coffee yet.

"In the fridge," Mom says. I fill a glass of ice and pour in the strong, black tea.

I eat my honeyed biscuits and eggs quickly so I can get back out into the fresh, cool morning. I gulp the last of my tea and pull on my boots and coat and head for the corrals to catch my horse. I breath the spring-smelling air and rejoice that one early bird, the turtle dove, is calling somewhere, giv-

46

ing his "ou OU ou ou ou" echolike call. He is probably quite close, but they always sound far away.

"Hey boy, can I catch you this morning?" I ask Gazelle, as he runs to the far side of the corral.

I approach him gently, and he takes the bit meekly, arching his Arabian neck proudly. I feel pride well up inside me. My horse. I trained him and look how he responds. I lead him to the tack room and slide the saddle into place, cinching it snug but not too tight.

Dad, already saddled up, swings aboard Lucy, who dances nervously. Her side has healed, leaving only a slight scar. Redwing, Mom's horse, stands quietly while Mom adjusts her tie-down. I adjust my martingale and swing lightly aboard. Gazelle steps out jauntily, his ears pricked up, ready for another day.

The cattle have scattered since last night, and we split up, looking in every possible draw and corner, spooking them out in the early gray light. The air now carries the smell of sage and cedar, and if the wind blows right, pine from the far-off Big Horns.

It's getting lighter now, a bit easier to make out cattle and horses. Bernard, Linda, and Sheila have arrived, and I hear their "Ge ups" and war whoops before I see them.

By the time the lazy sun starts to turn the sky blue-white and line the sunrise clouds with silver, the cattle are snaked out along the trail. They make a dark green trail through the grass as their feet knock the dewdrops off. The untrod grass is silver with dew.

The riders are in their favorite positions, according to theirs and their horses' skill. Dad rides point, the best position, leading the cattle and opening the gates. Bernard and Linda follow at the shoulder of the herd, keeping the front cattle moving and in line. Dean Floate, who joined the drive this morning when Bernard and Linda did, rides flank, across from me, to keep the cattle in line. Mom and Sheila bring up the rear, riding drag.

The herd reaches the crest of the hill, and I can see the Big Horn Mountains in all their splendor, with the snow-fields turning to silver and the mountains to an almost sky blue. I rein up for a moment, as I always do, just to look at the Big Horns' beauty. They are as much a part of the trip as the cattle and the yelling riders. This is the best time of the day. I hear a meadowlark and see the blue flirt of a mountain bluebird before I turn to push up the cattle.

By seven, we reach the corrals, where we will brand. The corrals are far away from the ranch buildings, in the middle of the summer pasture. By branding out here, we don't have to trail the newly branded calves from one pasture to another. They can stay here until fall and weaning.

The cattle balk and mill at the gate. The lead cows turn back to look for trailing calves, shouldering into the herd and causing confusion. The men cuss, and Gazelle and I rush back and forth from the shoulder of the herd to the drag, pushing the cattle and charging after the unruly ones who break and run.

"Get 'em, boy," I tell my horse, squeezing my legs tight against his sides. A cow dodges and twists, Gazelle following her every move like a shadow. One last dodge for freedom and she turns and runs back to the herd. The cattle finally submit and are trailing through the gate. My legs feel weak as I dismount and pat Gazelle's sweating neck. "Good boy."

We all relax for a moment, letting the cattle settle down a little, then we mount up again and push them into the smaller corral where the cows and calves will be separated.

Here the footmen take over. I unsaddle Gazelle and turn him loose in the larger corral before I run to help them. Now I'm a cutting horse, running and dodging to keep the calves from following their mothers out the gate. My throat is dry and my legs feel heavy. Still more to do. I run after one calf,

48

but he won't turn. To avoid being knocked down, I swerve, and Bernard, at the gate, turns him.

The cows out, we run the calves into the crowding pen, a smaller plank pen, to await their brands. Dad lights the propane heater to heat the irons and we settle back to relax for a moment while the irons heat. The only sound is the bawling of the calves and the bellowing of the cows.

Linda and Sheila jump into the crowding pen to push the calves into the calf table, which is similar to a squeeze chute, except that after the calf is caught, the table can be pulled out flat, laying the calf down so the brand can be easily and quickly applied.

Linda pushes a calf in, and Dad and Dean pull up on the two levers on the side, capturing the calf with iron bands around his neck, shoulder, and flank. The men pull down on the levers as one, and the table folds out, laying the calf out on his side.

I grab for an iron, and the hot metal burns through a hole in my leather glove and hurts my hand. I move my hands farther up on the iron to find a cooler spot and stamp the brand expertly on the calf's heaving side.

Branding, or handling the irons, is the elite job of the crew, and I am glad that I can do it. A brand has to be put on just right, without smearing or hair-branding, which is branding without leaving a scar. A hair-branded calf will show no sign of a brand in two or three months and can be easily rustled.

This elite position didn't come easily. When I was young, I would tally, or mark the calf down in a tally book as he was branded. This gave us an idea how many we branded each year and how many were heifers and how many were steers. As I got older, tallying was too tame, and I began to work in the crowding pen, where Linda and Sheila are now. That's the dirtiest job of the crew, and the hardest work. The

49

calves are big and have to be manhandled to get them into the chute.

From the crowding pen I was moved up, (or down) a notch to hind foot holder, holding the kicking hind leg out of the way of the person who castrates the bull calves. Holding the hind foot is dirty too, as the calves tend to be a little loose boweled this time of year. It is also nerve-wracking; if the foot slips out of your hold, it could mean a cut finger for the castrater.

The next calf in the table is a bull, and, as the crew is a little shorthanded, Bernard nods for me to take the hind leg. Dean, the other brander, can handle both irons for this calf. The U Milliron brand is formed by two separate irons, a U iron and a ⟨ iron.

I grab the hind leg, ducking out of the way of the stream of manure directed at me. The calf is big, and he kicks and struggles, testing my strength. I grip until my arm muscles hurt with the strain. "Don't let go," Bernard warns. "I want to keep my fingers."

I keep a tight hold, knowing he is depending on me. Finally, I can let go, and we turn the calf out of the chute. He jumps out, shaking his head and bawling for his mother.

The next calf is a heifer, and I grab the hot iron again, pressing it carefully down on the calf's side. "Careful," Dean says, "you'll burn that calf."

"Funny." I grin at him. The branding smoke boils up, hot and acid. It smells of singeing hair, and it makes my eyes water.

The morning seems endless, and it seems like the number of calves in the holding pen has hardly changed. "Beer break," Bernard says, so I know we are about half done. Linda Sue, my sister, is waiting in the pickup with the beer and pop.

The beer is cold, kept in coolers with chunks of ice. Although it is only near nine o'clock, we have been up since four, and the cold beer tastes good to our dusty mouths.

"How many have we done?" I ask Mom, who keeps the tally and handles the vaccine gun, giving the calves the blackleg vaccination. Blackleg is an infectious disease related to tetanus, and it can kill young animals.

Mom counts up the marks on the book. "Forty-two. Nineteen heifers and twenty-three steers."

"Took us forty-five minutes," Dad says, looking at his watch.

"Back to work," Bernard says, after about ten minutes. We still have about fifty calves to go.

The morning is hotter now, and the position between the calf table and the branding fire is sweltering. Sweat runs off my face and trickles down my back, tickling. Finally, the pen is almost empty. One last calf, and we will be done for today. The first day of branding will be over.

We have another beer, then saddle up again for the ride home. Joining the men on the ride home used to be the only part of branding I could do. Now I am considered a regular member of the crew. Dad, tired of riding, throws his saddle in the back of the pickup and turns his horse loose. She will follow Gazelle and Redwing back to the house.

Mom and I ride side by side, watching Bernard and Linda ride for their trailer at the pasture gate. They will join us later for dinner.

"Remember when we used to eat over here?" I ask Mom. We used to bring a propane camp stove, and Mom would fix lunch in the cabin near the corrals. "We always had hamburger gravy." Mom nods, turning Redwing toward home.

51

SUMMER

IT'S COLD THIS MORNING, but it usually is this early in the day. The sun is barely up, turning the sky orange-yellow in the east. This is the best time of the day to ride. Nothing can compare with the feeling of galloping along a high ridge just as the sun begins to light up the Big Horn Mountains in their coat of snow. The sun touches the hilltops, leaving the valleys below in undulating shadows.

A deer jumps out in front of us, and my horse shies delicately sideways. Laughing, I guide her back onto the trail. The deer bounds away, his antlered head, horns still in spring velvet, held high and proud.

The grass is still dew-wet, and the deer and my horse leave dark green trails through it as their hooves knock the white dewdrops off the grass. The dewy grass looks white under the sun, but soon the heat will burn off the dew, leaving the grass green and brilliant.

Below us I can see the windmill, catching the first rays of sunlight in its vanes. The top makes a golden whirl as the breeze catches it. The windmill waters the cattle when the small pond

above is dry during the summer. The rest of the pasture is dark.

On the county road running past the windmill a truck rumbles by, bearing the lattice-like steel tower that will be used in the oil drilling rig. Each year oil companies lease surface rights to ranchers' land, drilling test holes to discover oil-bearing strata. Many summers are filled with trucks and heavy equipment digging out new roads across the pasturelands and drilling test holes in the search for black gold.

The companies pay for the surface damages; they also pay a fee for each test hole they drill. Many years the money comes in mighty handy, especially when the cattle market is low. The roads the companies build out across the pastures come in handy for feeding cattle and for use during hunting season.

So far, for all the test holes, they have found no oil here, but several ranchers on Crazy Woman Creek to the south of us and on Powder River to the east have realized the dream of having a black monster pumping up oil from their lands, bringing almost instant wealth.

The sun is higher now, its golden light flowing down the hillsides. In the valley, the ranch buildings are still lying snug in the shadows. The light morning breeze carries up the crowing of a rooster and the bawl of a hungry calf. It must also carry the smell of the other horses, waiting in the corral, because Catawba, the horse I'm riding today, suddenly whinnies, the high-pitched sound echoing across the valley. From the corrals the other horses answer.

Finding a steep trail down, we drop off the ridge, down into the shadowed valley. The grass is still green and lush, but it will soon be burned to a buff-gold color by the summer sun.

It's colder down here than it is in the sunlight, and the air smells damp. I let Catawba trot, a long, springing stride that makes her seem to float across the ground. A horned owl, surprised from his night's meal, flies up in front of us. Catawba, startled, stops suddenly, ears stiffly forward. I pat her neck and watch the owl fly away, up the shadowed valley.

Finding the trail up the hillside, we climb out of the draw and back into the sunlight again. Across the gravel county road from us a bunch of cattle are lying down next to the water tank. I rein Catawba toward it and ride over to make sure the tall, stately windmill is doing its job, keeping the three water tanks full. Seeing us, the cattle heave to their feet, wondering if it is time to move out. We'll move them later, to another pasture. The grass in this one is getting short, and it is hard to depend on the fickle Wyoming wind to keep the windmill pumping water for the cattle.

Down in the valley below the windmill, the tall swamp grass is intermingled with the yellow-green leafy spurge plants and tall stickery Canada Thistle. Soon we will have to spray this to give the grasses a chance to grow.

Above me I hear an airplane, flying low. I look up, searching the blue sky. With a roar, the sprayer plane, hired to spray sagebrush in the back pastures, leaps the hill, circles above us, and disappears in the direction from which it came.

Catawba shakes her head, pulling at the bit, impatient to get home. I give her rein, and she walks up the hill, stopping at the gate to let me open it. I remount and turn her head to-ward home.

Back at the house, Mom and Dad are having hot coffee. I pour myself a cup and join them at the round kitchen table.

"How'd your horse go today?" Mom asks. Catawba is young yet and could be prone to buck.

"Fine. She didn't give me any trouble. We didn't go very far."

"You check the well?" Dad asks, referring to the windmill.

55

"Yeah, there's still lots of water. The windmill was pumping too."

"Maybe we'll take our horses up this evening and push some of the cows into the association pasture. There's more grass over there." Dad is referring to our biggest pasture, used for summer pasture. We call it the association because it was purchased many years ago from the Sheridan County Stockgrowers Association.

"About what time? Around three or four?" I ask, knowing that's when most of the cattle come in for water.

"Yeah, about three-thirty," Dad nods.

The summer evenings are long. With daylight saving time, it stays light until almost nine o'clock. We saddle up, glancing at the bank of black, evil-looking storm clouds moving slowly this way.

"We'll trailer up," Dad suggests. "It will save time, and we might get done before we get wet."

The clouds have moved in by the time we get up to the pasture, and the wind has come up, smelling of rain.

"Should we go ahead or wait?" Dad gives us the choice.

"Let's go. We'll just get wet, we've been wet before." I swing up on Catawba, heading her toward the windmill. Dad rides off to clear any cattle out of the rough draw to our right. Mom joins me, and we push the cows up the hill to the left along the fence line, pushing them toward the gate about a mile away.

Tiny wet drops hit my face, and the wind blows harder. The cattle move out, trotting, eager to go somewhere. The calves buck and kick, full of energy. Lightning splinters across the sky, followed by the sharp, loud crack of thunder. Catawba jumps and skitters, but she calms down as I pet her neck and talk to her.

"This ridge isn't the best place to be right now," I yell to Mom. "The metal on our tack could attract lightning."

56

I push Catawba into a trot to hurry the cattle off the high ridge and down into a shallow draw. The lightning splits the sky but stays in the upper atmosphere. I don't see any bolts attracted to the earth. Still, it isn't a good idea to make a target of oneself.

Often, lightning hits the dry summer grasses, starting prairie fires that sweep before the wind, leaving charred, black curls. Last fall, lightning hit our haystack, destroying several thousand dollars worth of hay before Dad, my brother-in-law Mike Lovato, and the Clearmont fire department could get it put out.

Catawba skitters as a crack of thunder echoes across the valleys. We have to push the cattle up over another ridge now and through the open gate. From the ridge we can see a streak of whitish cloud moving toward us from the north. In between the thunder crashes I can hear a deep roaring sound, like a freight train.

"Hail, coming up the valley," Mom yells, riding faster to push the rest of the cattle through the gate.

"Crumbs," I tell my horse. "I was only expecting rain, not hail."

I've been out in hailstorms before. Most of the hailstones are small, but they still hurt when driven by the angry wind.

The rain hits before the hail. The tiny wet drops grow bigger, and the wind splatters them over us. Rain begins to run off Catawba's mane, making it dark and stringy. It wets her neck and makes her chestnut coat dark. My own hair is stringy and wet under my headband, and my overall jacket clings to me wetly.

Mom, her dark hair straight with the rain, rides up beside me.

"You want to go back to the trailer or ride over to help your Dad?"

"Let's go help Dad. We can't get any wetter, anyway."

57

For a moment, the rain quits, and there is a lull in the wind. Then the hail hits, tiny ice pellets pinging off the ground like tiny ping pong balls. The hail is small, but the force with which it hits my hands and face makes each tiny pellet sting.

Catawba tries to turn her back to the storm, trying to get her face away from the stinging pellets. I let her swing sideways to get some relief. Head down, she plods into the storm, trying to stop in the shelter of a high bank to wait it out.

"There's Wallace, he's heading this way," Mom says.

"Let's go back to the trailer, that's where he's headed." I turn Catawba's head back toward the pickup and trailer. The rain and hail have almost quit now, but the wind blowing through my wet clothing is cold. I let Catawba trot and then canter back to the pickup, letting her pick her own way across the slippery wet ground.

Dad meets us back at the trailer.

"We got wet." He grins.

"Just a little," Mom laughs. "Did you find any cows?"

"I pushed some that way, they went out the gate, so I came back."

"You want us to shut the gate tomorrow?"

"No, we'll just leave it open. They can graze back in here if they want, but I wanted to get them out to the association to use that water hole so the old fools won't bog down in this one."

The horses are loaded, and the pickup feels warm. The sky is clearing now, the clouds moving away up the valley. If we had waited another half hour, we wouldn't have gotten wet.

HAYING

When Wyoming was a vast expanse of open range, uncut by fences, the ranchers let the cattle roam free in the
winter and rustle their own food. Now, with irrigation
and smaller ranches, hay is an important part of the
cattle industry. Many ranches have a great many acres
of hay land, but we have only a few. Still, the process
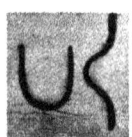 of irrigating, haying, and stacking of the
hay is much the same throughout Wyom-
ing. Modern technology is bringing in
newer and better ways to help ranchers,
such as huge sprinkler systems that re-
place the ditch method of irrigation and newer ways to
bale hay, making it less of a chore.

On the U Milliron, we still irrigate with shovel
and ditches and use both large round bales and the
older method of small square bales of hay.

Haying is an all-year job, or at least an all-
summer job, keeping ranchers busy from May until
August. Many times, with equipment breaking down,
wintertime is used to repair the equipment for the next
summer.

The Clear Creek Valley is hazy with smoke today; ranchers up the creek are burning the section of the main irrigation ditch that runs through their land. Each rancher has water rights to the ditch water and can use an allotted amount of water each summer for his hay or pasturelands. Every spring the main ditch is burned to clear old grass and weeds so the water can flow freely and so that weeds and grass will not pile up under bridges or culverts to obstruct the flow.

We have to burn our section of ditch today. It is about a mile long, winding around between the highway and the railroad track. I see Dad coming down the highway in the green and white pickup, loaded down with a spray tank full of water in case the fire gets out of control. Mom is driving the other ranch pickup loaded with shovels, rakes, and pitchforks as well as cans of gasoline and diesel fuel. A cooler full of food and drinks waits for lunch in the pickup bed.

Mom and I start burning at one end, with a can of diesel fuel and a box of matches. There isn't too much swamp grass here, but there are a lot of dried tumbleweeds. Mom and I rake them into a pile in the middle of the ditch and douse them with diesel fuel. Mom lights a match and tosses it on the pile. The flames shoot up, and the heat is too intense to let us stand very close. With a crackly sound, the tumbleweeds are soon reduced to a pile of ashes. Dad is working up from the other end of the ditch, hoping we'll all get done with the burning a little quicker. A car drives up and stops. It's Mike Lovato coming to lend a hand. Mom sends him up to help Dad on the other end.

Farther down the ditch is swamp grass, hanging over the sides of the ditch like loose-piled hay. By throwing a little diesel fuel on it and adding a little more where the grass is thin, the fire burns along the bank nicely. By doing both sides at once, the burning goes faster. It's a good plan, as long as no one has to walk down the bottom of the ditch between the rows of flame. The fire, fanned by a tiny breeze, begins to burn out of the ditch and across the meadow. I jump out of the ditch and use my rake to beat out the tongues of fire that curl up the bank. It is cooler up here, with the very slight breeze blowing the smoke away.

Up the ditch is a head gate with a check board beside it. The head gate opens to let water into the smaller ditches, and the check boards are used to raise the water level so more runs out the head gate. The wind has blown this area full of tumbleweeds, so I drop back down into the ditch to rake them up for burning. Even through my leather gloves I can feel blisters beginning on my hands from the rake handle, and my arms soon tire of the constant heaving motion of piling up the weeds. Finally, the weeds are piled up. There is a gasoline can and matches in the pickup; Dad and Mike are using a propane torch. I soak the pile with gasoline and make sure the can is moved a safe distance away before striking a match and throwing it on the pile. The gas-soaked weeds whoosh up in flames, and I have to move even farther back from the searing heat. Gasoline is dangerous to use, requiring very careful handling. People have been killed or have lost hands when carrying cans of gas too close to open flame. Still, it works very well to start fires on damp or green foliage.

The morning is long and hot. The sun is warm, and working near the open flame is hot work. By lunchtime, we have burned almost half the ditch, and we are ready for the sandwiches and iced tea and pop Mom packed this morning. While we're eating, the fire burns down the ditch, and some of it escapes and rushes through the dry grass in the field.

Lunch is postponed while we grab shovels, rakes, and the sprayer hose on the spray tank to fight the fire. The wind comes up a little stronger and whips the fire toward the sprayer pickup. Dropping my shovel, I run back to move the pickup a safe distance away. I hurry back to the fire line, where Mike is spraying the flames with water. The smoke billows up blackly against the sky, choking me and making my eyes water.

"It does this every year," Mom says, pounding the flames with her shovel.

"Right at lunch time, too," Dad adds.

The fire begins to retreat under our onslaught, breaking out in little rebellious patches when we think we have it out.

"The grass is so thick the water can't reach the fire," Mike says, spraying the dense, matted stuff.

"I know. The fire creeps along underneath. Last year we almost burned down an REA pole and a cottonwood tree. The REA frowns on people burning down their poles," I tell him. "The poles are soaked in creosote, and it burns pretty well."

Finally, the flames are driven back, and the burned area has formed a firebreak, so we can eat lunch without worrying too much about the fire getting away. After lunch, Mike takes the sprayer hose and does a little preventive spraying around the REA poles so we won't have to worry so much about them.

The rest of the ditch runs through rocky, barren soil, so there is little to worry about if it escapes the ditch. Leaning on rakes and shovels, we watch the flames eat along the ditch bank until they meet the area Dad has burned from the other end. Tomorrow, the ditch company will turn in the water, and the black ash will wash down the ditch and away.

Last night Dad told me to turn in the irrigation water, as the alfalfa field is probably getting dry. I dig out last year's irrigation dams, which are plastic sheets attached to two-by-

63

fours or poles five feet long. The pole lies across the ditch bank and the plastic spreads across the ditch to hold the water back. To keep the plastic from floating with the water, it must be weighed down with dirt and rocks.

The ground is hard to shovel, but I can scrape enough off to weigh down the dam. It takes several shovelfuls, and my shoulders and back are aching by the time I'm done. The dam looks like it will hold water. Across the highway is the main ditch with the head gate that has to be opened to let the water into our ditch. I turn the large wheel that opens the head gate and watch the water rush into the smaller ditch, carrying sticks and leaves with it. The rushing water hits my dam and trickles out underneath it. I pile more rocks and dirt on the dam until the trickle slows. It's hard to get a completely water-tight dam, so I leave it, watching the water spread out over the field.

The cold water feels good on my bare feet, clad only in rubber thongs. Dad wears irrigating boots, rubber boots that reach all the way to his waist. I have worn them, but I don't like the awkward feeling of walking in them. I like my thongs, and on a hot day the water feels good on my feet. Mom doesn't like thongs because there are often water snakes in the ditch. I don't mind them as long as they don't startle me.

The water rushes over the bank and spreads across the new seeding that Dad did last month. The earth is almost white until the water hits it, then it turns a deep wet brown. With the shovel I open up the breaks in the ditch bank, making them deeper and wider so the water can flow out easier. I watch it for a while longer to make sure it will flood this whole corner of the field. I set one more dam, farther down the ditch to catch this water when I turn it loose in about four or five hours, after the ground has soaked it up. By moving the dams a little ways down the ditch each time, the water will spread out and cover the whole field. Each set

64

is left for four to five hours or overnight to let the ground soak up as much as it needs to water the young plants.

The alfalfa is growing well. It stands about two feet high, with purple flowers above the green plants. The breeze sways them, and bees and butterflies rise off the plants. Soon it will be time to cut and swath and bale the hay for the winter.

In fact, the swather is sitting in my driveway right now, waiting for Dad and Bernard to get back from Buffalo with a belt and new canvases for it. The swather cuts and windrows the hay, all in one step. Some people use a mower to cut the hay and then a rake attached to a tractor to rake the hay into long piles, or windrows, so the baler can pick it up and mold it into a bale. The swather, a machine that looks something like a squat combine, does both. The swather blade cuts the hay and throws it up onto two canvas rollers that roll the hay into a hole between the canvases. The hay is then laid out in a neat row, ready for the baler.

Dad and Bernard drive in, and I go to help them.

"Did you find the belt?" I ask, knowing that parts are not always in stock when you need them.

"I got one that's an inch long, but I think we can make it work," Dad says. He's an expert at making things work.

"Want a beer?" Bernard offers me a cold can of Coors.

"Thanks." I watch them unload the canvases from the pickup.

"Now what?" I ask.

"Start unscrewing those bolts that hold the canvases on." Dad hands me a screwdriver. I'm pretty good at small jobs like that, and at fetching and carrying tools. Mechanics is not my calling, and I don't really like the dirty grease on the machines. Still, machinery is a part of ranch life too, and it's necessary to know some basic fix-it skills.

It takes nearly two hours to fix the swather, but we finally get it to run.

65

"Want to ride around the field a couple of times?" Dad asks.

The swather isn't made for two, so I have to stand on the small platform near the driver, hanging onto the railing. It isn't bad, except when Dad hits the turning brake to bring the swather around in a tight turn at the end of the field.

"Hang on," he yells over the engine noise. This is not to be taken lightly, and I almost fall off as he makes the turn. A cold shiver runs through me at the thought of falling in front of those big blades. The wind blows bits of dust and hay back into our faces, and I can see this will never be one of my favorite jobs.

But when alfalfa is cut, it perfumes the air like nothing else can. It is a sweet, grassy smell mingled with the spicy smell of the purple flowers. Every year, up and down Clear Creek Valley, one can smell the perfume in the air and know that haying season is here. I can smell it now on the early morning breeze, coming from the rows of hay Dad swathed, laid out to dry in the hot sun. Hay baled before it is properly cured will burn from the chemical reaction of the green hay as it decomposes. Sometimes this just leads to bad-tasting hay, but sometimes the heat generated can cause a haystack to burst into flame. It is a weird feeling to break open a bale of hay on a cold winter's day and feel heat inside, trapped since summer.

The next morning I'm up early, stepping out to look at the fresh morning sunlight and smell the freshcut hay. Clouds are boiling up over the mountains to the west, and I hope it doesn't rain. Although in this semiarid climate moisture is usually welcome, during the hay season ranchers pray for dry weather. Hay baled too wet will mold, and moldy hay fed extensively to pregnant cattle will cause them to abort the unborn calves.

The phone rings, dulled by distance. I debate about letting it ring, then go inside to see who's calling. It's Dad.

"Cynthy, think you can drive a stock truck with those big bales of hay? That way we can get done hauling a little faster."

"Sure. I'll be right out." I decide not to tell him I had an invitation to go up on the mountain today with a group of friends. I work for Dad, so I'm always on call.

He's waiting for me when I pull in, checking inside the stock truck to make sure there's plenty of oil in the engine.

"Where are we hauling hay from, Pitch's?" I ask, knowing they are buying hay from a neighbor up the creek, as our little bit of hayland is insufficient to raise enough hay to feed our cattle. Dad and Bernard bale the hay after Curtis Pitch swaths it. The U Milliron Company has recently purchased a baler that makes the big, round, 1000-pound bales. These are handled with hydraulic equipment attached to the pickup bed or with a tractor fitted with a grapple hook. Using this equipment, haying becomes a one-man operation.

Today we have to haul the baled hay from the field where it has been baled to our own stackyards, where it will wait for winter feeding. I am in charge of driving the smallest of the three trucks, which will haul five of the large bales. Dad's truck, fitted with a wooden extender on the truck bed, will haul six bales, and Bernard's new truck, with a twenty-four-foot bed, will haul up to sixteen.

Bernard is already loading hay when we reach the field, about nine miles away. The tractor and grapple hook, a rack-like thing with long teeth that grab the bale and hoist it into the air, looks like a prehistoric monster eating the huge bales for lunch.

I can see the Big Horn Mountains clearer from here, and the clouds are almost gone, leaving only white trails against the blue sky. The snow on the topmost peaks looks cool and inviting, and I wish I were there instead of sitting in the hot cab of the truck. I cut the engine and get out, joining Dad, who is lying under his truck in the shade.

"Hot already, isn't it?" Dad says, finding a likely looking piece of grass to whistle through, something I could never do.

"Yeah. Going to be hotter, looks like. How much hay did you buy?"

"Two-hundred ton. Think that's enough?"

"Should be," I answer. It all depends on the winter, though. In a bad winter, the cattle can eat a lot of hay.

Bernard has finished loading his truck, and the tractor scuttles across the field, looking for another bale to sink its huge teeth into. Back and forth, picking up bales and gently rocking my truck as they set down on the bed. It doesn't take long to load my truck, but I'll wait for Dad before pulling out.

Two more trucks pull into the lane and turn onto the field. It's some friends of ours from down on Crazy Woman Creek, coming to get hay. Bernard stops the tractor and comes over for a minute. "I'll load them up before you go, then you won't have to wait at the stackyard for me to come unload you."

Dad agrees, and we walk across the field to chat. Bernard loads their trucks and then begins loading Dad's. As our friends leave the field, carefully crossing the ditch between the field and the gravel road, the second truck wobbles, spilling the huge bales back onto the field. Bernard reloads the hay, and the truck rattles up the road.

The trucks loaded, we head carefully across the field. Dad crosses the ditch between the field and the road and waits to make sure I can cross alright. I brake carefully, cut the engine, and get out.

"You drive it across. I'm chicken." Dad maneuvers it across easily, going slowly and carefully. From now on the

68

going is easy, as most of the travel is on the highway or gravel road.

Bernard is unloading his truck when we pull up to the stackyard, using another tractor with a grapple hook. The hay piles up, the big round bales looking like giant jelly rolls lying side by side.

"This is the only way to load hay," Bernard says, stepping out of the air-conditioned tractor cab. That's easy for him to say. Our trucks don't have air conditioning, and it feels like a hundred degrees inside them. It is easier, though, than heaving the bales onto a pickup bed. Just four more trips, and we will be done hauling this cutting of hay. Tomorrow, Dad will bale the hay that is drying at my house, and we will load it and stack it the old-fashioned way, using good old manpower.

Mom, Dad, Mike, Linda, and I all turn out for the hot, heavy work of loading and stacking the small square bales of hay. Each bale weighs between forty and sixty pounds and has to be picked up off the field and stacked on the pickup. With two pickups and several hands, the job doesn't take too long.

Mom and Linda each drive a pickup. I do the stacking on one pickup while Dad and Mike toss the bales up to me. The pickup moves at a slow crawl, but balance is still tricky. I push and shove the bales into place, working fast to keep up with the two men. When one pickup is full, Mom and I go to unload while Dad, Mike, and Linda fill the other pickup.

The haystack in my driveway is tumbled down on one side, so Mom and I rearrange the weathered bales to make a steadier rest for the new ones. Stacking bales is rather an art. Each layer is alternated, with bales first going north and south, then east and west. Otherwise, the stacks will tumble down. Mom does the stacking while I hand her the bales off the pickup. There should be forty bales on a load, but I keep

69

a silent count so we'll know for sure how many we have. My leather gloves are hot on my hands, but I leave them on, knowing that the baler twine can be viciously sharp on bare hands.

"Boy, it's hot today," I comment. The sun is molten-looking in the blue sky, and I hope that the clouds hanging low over the mountains will head this way to cool things down. The sweat sticks to me, and there is no breeze to dry my wet face and sticky arms. The hay clings to me, itchy and annoying, and a spider dangles from my cap brim, looking me in the eye.

"It's humid too. Unusual for Wyoming," Mom says. "But just think how we'll complain about the cold this winter."

"That's Wyoming. Either too hot or too cold." We finish stacking and drive back to the field. Dad and Mike pull up to the stack to unload their hay. Linda drives our pickup while Mom and I load. This time I walk behind the pickup, heaving the bales up to Mom.

Four more trips back and forth, and we are finished. There should be enough hay to feed my small herd of Angus heifers come calving season. Haying is over for another year.

POISONING WEEDS

Leafy spurge was brought into the United States by the government as an ornamental plant to be displayed in the U.S. Botanic Gardens. European in origin, it is a pretty plant, with light green leaves and tiny yellow flowers on a tall stalk. In Europe, there is a beetle that eats spurge and controls its spread, so it does not become a problem. In the U.S., especially in the western states, it has. Although it was supposed to stay in the botanic gardens, no one told the spurge that, and it found habitat to its liking in the West.

Spurge is a fast-growing plant that grows best on irrigated lands, but it will also grow miles from surface water. It comes up in dense clumps, crowding out grass and other beneficial plants wherever it takes hold. The roots of the spurge plant bore into the ground for six feet or more, making it nearly impossible to pull or plow up. Each root sends out runners that travel under the ground from the main plant up to ten feet in all directions. From these runners, new plants emerge and repeat the cycle. Burning is ineffective, as the roots are not damaged. Cattle will not eat it, and it destroys valuable grazing lands if left unchecked. Poisoning spurge not only benefits the rancher and his livestock but wildlife as well, as they seldom eat spurge.

Fighting spurge, and to a lesser extent, thistle, is an all-summer job. The weed and pest officials have recently imported the spurge beetle to help fight the spurge, but until they are convinced that the beetle will not hurt beneficial crops, we fight spurge with Tordon 2K or Banval, powerful herbicides that will kill only broadleaf plants, not grass or grains. 2-4-D, a chemical poison used to kill sagebrush, is not strong enough to kill spurge. Tordon rarely kills it effectively the first year; often it takes several applications to get rid of the spurge.

Many times it is a discouraging job, as spurge you have poisoned two years in a row can still come back. But we have to keep fighting it to maintain the grasslands.

"Where are we going to spray today?" I ask Dad, taking a sip of my coffee.

"We'd better spray the ditch bank. The weed and pest people can see that from the highway."

"Right." We try to keep all of our spurge under control, but we especially like to kill that in plain sight. Then the weed and pest officials can see we are working on it. The spurge problem is getting bad enough that ranchers who won't try to control the spread of spurge on their property can be ordered by the court to control it or be subjected to a fine. The weed and pest department helps by paying for half of the poisons used, but the spraying is still expensive.

The spray tank on the pickup is filled with water and Tordon concentrate and is ready to go. Dad checks the gas in the sprayer's motor and fills the two-gallon gas can that we carry with us for refueling the sprayer pump engine.

It's going to be a hot day. At only 8:30 A.M., the thermometer reads eighty degrees. At least we won't have to walk much with the spray rig. Most of the spraying can be done from the pickup, sitting on the tailgate and operating the hose from there. Along the irrigation ditch, the spurge is thick and dense, with green and yellow flowers waving in the slight breeze. Sometimes the ditch company sends people to spray the spurge on this main ditch, but for this year it is up to each rancher to control the spurge on his length of ditch.

The ditch water is dirty, but it looks cool on a hot day. When I was a kid, my friends and I used to play in the ditch, and even now I sometimes enjoy a dip in the cold water of the creek on a hot day.

Dad pulls the cord to start the motor, which is much like the ones used on lawn mowers. The engine starts, and the long hose curls like a snake as the spray throbs through it. Dad motions for me to sit on the tailgate, and he gets behind the wheel, driving slowly so I can swing the nozzle back and forth to wet all the spurge. My arm begins to tire, the

74

muscles rebelling against the weight of the spray nozzle and the uncomfortable position. After a time, Dad stops the pickup and comes back to relieve me, letting me drive along the narrow ditch bank, which is hardly wide enough for a pickup.

I glance occasionally in the rearview mirror, and I haven't driven very far before Dad waves for me to stop.

"Come here. I want to show you something." I jump out, wondering what Dad has in mind. "Look." He points to the right tires of the pickup, only inches away from the edge of the ditch, where the bank drops sharply off into the four-foot-deep water.

"You're a little close to the edge," Dad says.

Shaken, I let him drive. I could have tipped us all into the ditch, possibly getting one of us badly hurt and wrecking the pickup. I'm shorter than Dad, so it's harder for me to see across the right side of the pickup. I try not to think about it as I continue to spray.

Dad stops the pickup near a large patch of spurge, off the ditch bank in a small hollow. There is too much spurge to spray while the pickup is moving, so I have to drag the hose down into the patch to cover the plants with enough spray to kill them. Sitting on one of the plants is a black and yellow Monarch butterfly, fanning his magnificent wings. I don't want to spray him; his wings might become too wet for him to fly. Carefully, I slide my fingers under him and lift him off the plant. Unafraid, the butterfly sits for a moment on my finger, then lifts off into the sky, looking for other plants.

It takes all morning to finish the ditch bank, and after a filling meal of beans, ham, and cornbread we go back out to spray a patch of spurge along Clear Creek.

"Lot's of spurge here, isn't there?" Dad asks, pointing to a shady swale near the creek. The meadow is full of the yellow-green spurge. Even though we have sprayed it here for five years, it keeps coming back. It is discouraging to feel that each year the money and effort that was put into trying to rid an area of the stuff was futile. We can't give up, though, and have to keep going over places year after year until finally the spurge is gone.

"We poisoned heavy here last year. Look at the sterilized soil here." I point to some patches of bare ground, which are even free of grass. Although Tordon is supposed to kill only broadleaf plants, a too-heavy application will kill everything, and it takes plants up to two years to re-establish.

Dad starts the engine, and I jump on the tailgate to start another round of spraying. A mosquito hums near my ear, and I'm glad I remembered to use insect repellent before I left. I have several itchy welts left over from this morning, when I forgot the repellent. No matter how hot it is, the mosquitos along the creek are vicious. In the cool evening, they are unbearable. Now they circle around my head, buzzing, but are unwilling to bite through my repellent shield.

The spray blows in my face, tasting bitter. Sometimes I wear a dust mask over my nose and mouth, but it is uncomfortable and makes breathing difficult. I don't really know how dangerous Tordon exposure might be, but for today I'm willing to let the future take care of itself and hope that I'm not doing my body any lasting harm.

Dad swings the pickup closer to the creek and stops so I can drag the hose to a large patch of spurge behind a pile of dirt. A bubble rises in the hose next to the nozzle. Before I can reach the engine to turn it off, the bubble breaks, spraying my face and upper body with the bitter-tasting spray.

My eyes sting, and I spit the stuff out of my mouth, trying not to swallow. The creek is close by, so I drop face down into the creek, letting the cold water wash over my face. Opening my eyes to let the water wash through them, I see swaying green seaweed and mossy rocks. The name Clear Creek is a misnomer. Clear Creek is full of dirty brown water, but I let some of it run into my mouth, to rinse out the foul Tordon. The water tastes of old fish, but at the moment it is the lesser evil. The bitter taste doesn't leave, but I think most of the Tordon is washed out.

Dad chuckles when I emerge, my hair plastered to my head and hanging in dripping strands to my shoulders. My shirt front clings damply to me, wet and smelling of Tordon. Dad is concerned too. "You okay? Did you swallow any?"

"No. I got to the creek quick enough to wash it out of my eyes and mouth."

"How does it taste?" Dad asks.

"Like it smells. Bad."

Dad checks the hose, patched in several other places with black tape. "Well, we can't spray anymore until I get a new hose. This one's about had it."

"We put in three hours this afternoon. Time to quit anyway." It doesn't take long for me to get tired of spraying.

"Tomorrow we can take some beads up in that draw we saw some in last week, when we scattered tubs," Dad says. "Maybe your mom will want to go along."

Spraying is basically a two-person job, but for beading we need all the hands we can get. Especially in the rough country Dad is referring to. We were up on the ridge above it last week, with a mineral mix we put out for the cattle. There was a lot of spurge in places where the pickup can't go.

Mom enjoys getting outside, and she and Dad are loading the pickup when I drive up the next day. The beads are actually little brown pellets, about an eighth-inch long, made of Tordon. They work on the root of the plant, soaking into the ground. They are packaged in round barrels of cardboard that weight about fifty pounds each. So far Dad and Mom have ten barrels on the pickup.

"How many will we need?"

77

" 'Bout twenty," Dad answers. "It may take a lot of beads."

I see that the beaders, actually grass seeders used to throw the beads in a wide arc, are already loaded. We take four; in case one breaks down we have an extra. Each beader holds about twenty-five pounds of beads and is carried around our shoulders by means of an adjustable canvas strap.

The canyon is too steep and rugged to drive into, so from the top of the ridge we have to carry the beads down to the spurge patchs. It is hard to carry the fifty-pound barrels down the steep hill without being overbalanced, so we lay the barrel at the edge of the draw and let it roll down. They don't break too often before coming to rest at the bottom of the hill.

Filling my beader at the pickup, I head down the hill after my barrel to bead a large patch of spurge. Dad is still filling his beader, and Mom has already disappeared around a turn in the narrow trail. Suddenly, near my foot, I hear a sharp "Ruzzzz" sound. I jump back, having heard enough rattlers to know the sound. The snake buzzes angrily at me again for disturbing him and starts winding away. We'll have to keep watch; where there is one snake it's likely there will be more. I wave at Dad, keeping an eye on the snake.

"Snake," I yell up to him, and he brings a posthole shovel to kill it. He cuts off the rattles and puts them in his shirt pocket. It is a large snake, with ten buttons. "Alvin Betz used to kill them by grabbing their tails and snapping them like a whip. Snapped the heads off. He quit it after one's head didn't snap off, and it just missed getting him on the cheek," Dad tells me.

"You won't catch me doing that." Snakes don't really bother me, and even rattlers don't send me into a panic. Our prairie rattlesnakes are small, seldom stretching more than four feet in length. As a rattler's venom potency is in direct

78

proportion to its size, the prairie rattler is probably the least dangerous of all poisonous snakes. Still, I wouldn't care to be bitten by one.

The snake is forgotten as the work goes on. We agree not to tell Mom. She doesn't like any snake, and rattlers least of all.

My beader runs out of beads after only fifteen minutes of work. At the moment I am closer to the pickup than I am to the barrel I rolled down the hill, so I clamber back up the hillside to refill. The loose dirt makes it hard to climb up, but going back down is easy. I can slide most of the way.

I come to a deep washout filled with spurge and coarse swamp grass. I slide down the steep sides and crank the beader, sending a spray of beads pattering over the grass and weeds. Above the pattering noise of the beads hitting grass and the clicking of my beader I hear another sound. Not a rattler this time, but something that sounds like a hissing cat.

Occasionally our barn cats will go wild and roam the hills, catching mice and rabbits and escaping foxes and other predators. This draw opens near the house, so maybe there is a barn cat hiding in the grass.

I walk toward the sound and can hear the animal spitting angrily at me. Framed by the tall grass is a wild, furry face, bigger even than Checko, Mom's huge house cat. The face is spotted and brown, not the light orange-brown of a domestic cat, but the dark tan color of a bobcat.

The bobcat hisses again, the eyes round and yellow, the ears flat against the head. For all it's furious spitting and hissing, the eyes show fear. I can tell by the extra-large ears and smaller paws that this is a kitten, and there is undoubtedly another one behind it in the den. It looks very much like my own kittens, only much bigger.

Mama Bobcat is probably around somewhere. Having no need to disturb the kitten further, I back away, up the hill, wishing I had my camera. I hate to carry it when I'm using Tordon, as the herbicide corrodes metal. It would have been nice to have along today; we seldom see bobcats on the ranch. I have seen lots of tracks, but this is the first time in twenty years I have seen one in the wild. When I was about four years old, we came home late one night and saw a group of four kittens playing on the county road, the first bobcats I had ever seen.

I bead up and down the cuts, working my way back to where Dad is working. He has carried several barrels of beads from the pickup so we can refill without having to climb back up the hill. My beader is empty by the time I reach him.

"Look." He points up the hillside, and it takes me a minute to see the tan blur of a furry body leaping up the hillside. A bobcat, a little bigger than the kitten I saw, disappears over the ridge.

"That must be the mother. I saw a kitten down in the draw. I'll bet there was another one behind it in the den."

"I kinda like to see a few of them around," Dad says, pouring beads into my beader. "We used to never see them."

"I know. I remember those in the road that night. There must be more of them around, or else we can just get around more."

Watching for more bobcats as I bead, I daydream and get too close to the edge of a cutbank. The dirt has been undermined by washing water, and the crumbly dirt gives way beneath my feet. For a brief second I am airborne, then my shoulder hits the dusty earth, and I roll down the short slope. The beader slams into my arm, and the dust fills my mouth, tasting gritty and earthy. I wonder if I'll roll all the way to the draw bottom, about twenty feet down. I can't get a foothold or a handhold on the loose dirt. I feel a jar as I hit a hard branch of greasewood. It jams painfully into my back but holds my weight. I watch the blue sky spin for a minute,

80

then I pull myself to my feet. I untangle my beader, surprised that I haven't lost many beads.

Dad is looking over the edge at me. "You okay?"

One leg hurts, and my back and side feels bruised, but everything still works. "Yeah. The bank gave way."

"You should know better than to get that close to the edge."

I shake the dirt off my pant leg. "That's where daydreaming gets me," I grin at Dad, and try to find a way back up out of the cut. The soreness disappears as we keep working. Uphill, down in the draw, and back for more beads. By one o'clock the thousand pounds of beads are scattered over the acres of spurge, and we can go home and shade up for the rest of the day.

Fencing

Before the coming of the homesteaders, the Wyoming range land was open, uncut by fence lines. Cattle roamed freely, and each year roundups were held, one in the spring to brand the new calves, and one in the fall to wean and gather animals for sale. Notices were posted as to the boundaries and dates of each drive by the stockgrowers associations, and ranchers could send their representatives to help with the gather and to brand the rancher's calves.

The homesteading act that went into effect in 1862 ended the open range era. Fences began to crop up to protect homesteader's plots and farm crops. The blizzard of 1887 went a long way toward convincing ranchers that fencing might be useful for the cattle industry. With fences, cattle could be kept close to the buildings during the winter and fed dryland hay, reducing the risk of starvation and predation. Cows could be watched closer during calving season, and those having trouble could be helped, saving cow and calf. Ranchers could breed cows to better bulls and upgrade the herds. Maximum use of grazing land could be obtained by rotating pastures, allowing for reseeding of native grasses while cows grazed elsewhere.

The problem was what materials to use. Trees for poles were few in Wyoming, so in 1887 when barbed or bob wire was introduced, it offered an inexpensive alternative. The first barbed wire was wicked looking wire, with huge, ragged chunks of metal wrapped around a strand of wire. It was certain injury to anything that ran afoul of it, and even the tough-hided longhorns soon learned to turn from it.

Through the years, barbed wire has become more refined, with smaller barbs. Today, the most common type in Wyoming is two pieces of wire, twisted together, with a sharp, pointed barb wrapped around one ply of the wire at about six-inch intervals. This wire holds cattle fairly well and will not rip through their tough hides. Horses can and sometimes do get badly cut in wire, but for cattle it is inexpensive, practical fencing material.

Squirt sits comfortably on my lap, kneading her claws into my leg.

"Let's go fix that fence in the windmill pasture today," Dad says, coming around the corner from the hall and going through the kitchen to his den.

I glare at his retreating back. Fence fixing is not one of my favorite ranch chores, and sometimes I wish the whole of Wyoming was open range again. Still, fencing has to be done, and after fifteen years of ranching I am becoming proficient at digging postholes, stretching wire, and stapling it back up.

I try to push Squirt off my lap, and she responds by digging her claws into my leg to hang on. I detach her and drop her on the floor. Giving me a dirty look, she zooms away, sliding on the slick wood floor.

Outdoors, Dad finds some fence pliers and loads some fence posts and a roll of wire into the back of the pickup. I find the post pounder for the steel posts, the wire stretchers, staples, and steel post clips.

"How do we get to the fence to fix it?" I ask, climbing into the pickup. The section of fence that we have to fix has been flattened by a landslide and is on a steep hillside. I know the pickup can't climb up the hill to the fence, but maybe we can come in from above the section of fence by cutting off the ridge road and driving down the steep hillside.

The ridge road is fairly smooth, but when Dad turns the pickup off into the sage, the truck jerks and bounces. The hillside Dad hopes to drive down is a network of washed-out ditches, cutbanks, and upthrustings of sandrocks. It looks too steep to drive down.

"That's a long walk down," I comment, thinking of having to lug the steel posts, wooden posts, and post pounder down the hill to where the fence needs fixing. It's about an eighth of a mile walk.

84

"We can get down. Just have to be careful of the ditches." The track he proposes is barely wide enough for the pickup and is lined on both sides by deep, rough ditches. If we slide the pickup into one of these, we could easily tip over.

"We can't get back up, but I think we can get down there." Dad never worries about the unimportant things. "You want to ride or walk down?"

"I'll ride. I can always close my eyes."

Dad eases the pickup down the hill, watching carefully on both sides, keeping to the middle as much as possible. The pickup hits some soft sand, and the back end begins sliding sideways toward a deep drop-off.

"You're sliding," I tell Dad needlessly. I expect to feel the jolt of the pickup tire falling off into the ditch any minute.

Dad puts on the brakes gently. "I wonder if we can make it without getting stuck?"

It does little good to worry about that now. The pickup doesn't have enough power in reverse to pull it back up the steep slope, and we would only spin the tires and slide more. We have to keep going down.

The ground looks terribly close to the windshield as the pickup nearly stands on it's grill at the bottom of the incline. "We'll probably bury the front end and somersault," Dad jokes. He can joke now, as the pickup levels out on the flatter ground at the bottom of the hill.

"This may be a foolish question, but how are we going to get out, now that we're here?" The hillside we have just come down is too steep to climb back up, and below us is a deep draw. The hillsides around us are steep and rutted.

"There's some spurge. I've got some beads in the back. Sprinkle some on it. " Dad nods to the patch of yellow-green foliage not far from the pickup. "I think we can drive around the head of the draw and up that swale and get back on the

85

ridge road," Dad says, pointing out the route. It looks possible. The land is flat between the edge of the draw and the hillside, and it looks wide enough for a pickup. The swale is a gradual slope up to the road.

I jump into the pickup bed to get the beads and beader to kill the patch of spurge. The box, which we left open, flipped upside down on the ride down the hill, and beads are spilled all over the pickup bed.

"We forgot to close the box. The beads spilled all over."

"Damn. I didn't even think to close the box. Well, you can get most of them," Dad says, opening the tailgate and pulling out two wooden posts and the shovel. Heaving them onto his shoulders, he heads up to start on the fence.

The beads are difficult to pick up by hand, lying as they do between the ridges in the pickup bed. I get most of them scooped up, and it doesn't take long to bead the patch of weed. When I finish that little chore, I grab two steel posts, some staples and clips and fence pliers, and follow Dad.

Dad is already at work digging a posthole in the hard, dry ground.

"Better bring all the steel posts. Looks like we'll need 'em." Dad looks up from his posthole long enough to survey the rest of the flattened fence.

"I hope we don't need more than five. That's all we brought."

"We'll make them do."

It takes two trips to bring up the steel posts and post pounder, a steel pipe half full of lead, used to pound the posts into the ground. The hollow end of the pipe is slipped over the post, and by pulling it up and then dropping it to let the weighted end hit the top of the post, the post is driven into the ground. Steel posts are good fencing material, being easy to drive and easy to work with, but they are not satisfactory for an entire fence, so we use wooden ones as well, set-

86

ting them deep into the ground. Steel posts are lighter in weight and smaller than wooden posts. If a cow hits a fence made entirely of steel posts, the posts will bend over. During winters of deep snow, steel posts can be driven into the ground two or three feet by heavy drifts. Wooden posts add stability to the fence. One wooden for every two or three steel posts seems to work about right.

Even with our new road down the hill, the pickup is still some distance from the fence, and I am sweating by the time I get the posts packed up to the fence.

Below me on the open grass field is a red spot, looking out of place among the summer-dry grass. It's a red fox, after field mice. He stands, head cocked, until he hears one under the grass. With a quick, bouncing spring, all four legs stiff, he pounces. The mouse must have eluded him, because he waits again, listening. Then the curled body and quick graceful pounce. He comes back up, his head high.

"A fox," I tell Dad. "I think he caught a mouse."

The fox must have heard me; he looks up. Seeing his audience, he takes off across the field, his bushy tail straight out behind him.

Dad looks up, catching a glimpse of the red streak below us.

"We never used to see many foxes around. There's getting to be more of them," he says, going back to his work.

"I know. When I was young, we never saw any at all. I'm glad they're coming back."

"Just so they stay out of the chickens," Dad says. Foxes can eat through a chickenhouse full of chickens in a hurry.

"You want me to start down here?" I ask, surveying the fence coming up the hillside.

"Yeah. Put in a steel post where you need one, but save two for me to use up here."

87

There are several places that could use posts, but I choose the three worst spots and set the post as close to the old posthole as possible, to keep them in line with the fence.

Dad, watching me lift the heavy pounder off the post and drop it down to drive the post into the ground, warns, "Be careful. Don't let the pounder get too high. It could slip off the post and give you a headache."

I work more cautiously after that and finish driving the posts in. The wire can't be clipped on the posts yet, as it is still attached to the post that is lying flat on the ground. The next job is to take the staples out of the down post, letting the wires pull back up. With the fence pliers, I begin to work on the post, pulling out staples from the weathered wood. One gives quicker than I expect it to, and the fence pliers fly up and graze my cheek. I touch the stinging spot and come away with blood on my fingers.

"What happened?" Dad asks.

"I wasn't expecting that staple to come loose so fast. The pliers got me."

"You gotta watch that."

"So I noticed."

Dad tamps his wooden post into the ground and then resets the one that has fallen over. "You tamp for a while." Dad hands me the shovel. It's hard to tamp on the hillside, as the dirt keeps sliding down the hill, away from the fence. I do the best I can, and finally the post is fairly tight.

"I can't get it any better," I tell Dad.

He wiggles it a little. "It'll hold until the next landslide."

It takes both of us to pull up the wire and staple it to the newly reset post. When we get the staples driven in, the wire is taut, making a good fence. Dad drives more staples into the other two wooden posts while I twist the post clips around the steel posts.

88

"Now we'll see if we can get out of here." Dad picks up some dry, weathered fence posts to take home for firewood, and I follow with the shovel, post pounder, and staple bucket.

The road Dad is making works well until we are almost to the top of the ridge. Blocking our way is a ledge of sand-rock too big for the pickup to climb over without high-centering. Between two of the rocks is a narrow alleyway. "I think we can go through there," Dad says.

The rock alley looks too narrow for anything as large as the pickup, but we hate to turn back so close to the road. We leave a streak of green paint along one rock as a mark of our passing, but we make it through.

"After lunch there's a gate I want to fix up in the meadow. It shouldn't take too long. We'll see if your Mom wants to go."

"She might. We may as well do it, while we've got everything in the pickup."

Mom has stew waiting for us when we get home. She pours me a tall glass of iced tea as we walk in.

"You should see the new roads we made today," I tell her.

"I'm just as glad I didn't." Mom isn't too fond of making new roads.

Between drinks of tea, I describe the roads in detail. "We'll probably never have to use them again."

After lunch, Mom declines the invitation to go back out with us, so Dad and I load up some more steel posts and head up the county road until we turn off to drive up the steep road to reach the gate. It's on a high, windswept ridge, and the post is loose because of the dirt caving away from around it. It's leaning inward, and the gate is sagging.

"We'll have to put in a dead man," Dad says. "Do you know what a dead man is?"

89

"Kinda. I don't know how to make one, though." It isn't as bad as it sounds. A dead man is a rock with wires twisted around it and buried in the dirt. By wrapping the other end of the wires around the post, the weight keeps it pulled up from one side.

"I'll show you," Dad says. He pulls up the sagging post, and I scoop some dirt in around it and tamp it down. "That will do for now. Cut me a piece of wire, about ten foot long." I cut the wire off the roll and bring it over. Dad loops the wire around the post and twists it together tightly.

"What kind of a rock do you need?"

"See if you can find one about two feet square, one that won't break or crumble."

That's a tall order. The hillside is littered with rocks, but most are sandstone, sedimentary rocks formed by layers of dirt pressed together over the centuries. Sandstone is soft, and the layers peel off and crumble easily. What I want is one of those rough, red rocks, formed long ago by volcanic action. They are lumpy enough to hold the wire and will not crumble or break easily. I find one several feet away and stagger back to Dad with it. I get a little close to the edge of the ridge and have to drop the rock until I can regain my balance on the loose shale that threatens to roll me down into the draw.

Dad has a deep hole dug in the hillside when I get back. He wraps the ends of the wire attached to the post around the rock and drops it into the hole. The rock should be heavy enough, when buried, to hold the post erect. Dad pulls the post up straight while I tamp the loose dirt on top of the rock, making it firm and packed.

"Seems like we ought to put up a tombstone," I joke. "After all, it is a dead man."

"He'll just have to lie in an unmarked grave," Dad grins.

90

The wind is coming up, and the sun is behind the cloud-bank to the west. It's cold up here where the wind isn't blocked by the ridges. My hair whips around my face and the wind tickles inside my ears. My light overall jacket isn't very warm.

"Good enough," Dad says, surveying the job. "Let's go home."

"I'm getting cold. Think it will rain tonight?"

"It never rains in Wyoming," Dad says facetiously. This time, Dad's right. The next day is sunny and cloudless.

"Shall we roll up that tangle of wire in the horse pasture today?" I ask, remembering the tangle of wire and posts that I rode around some days ago. Loose wire is a hazard to livestock, especially horses. Cattle, too, can get caught in it, but their thick hides don't get cut as easily as horses' do.

"We'll get that, then go over on the creek and roll up the wire around the old corral."

It takes about twenty minutes to finish the job in the horse pasture, but much of the wire near the creek is buried in dirt that has accumulated over many years. We pull what wire we can out of the ground, but some is buried too deep. This we cut close to the ground, leaving it to rust.

The wire we can get we roll into huge hoops that look like spiny hula hoops. Wire rolling is easy once you get the hang of it. The wire is started in a hoop shape, and each piece is woven back and forth over the next to hold it in place, rather resembling the crown of thorns. When one does enough wire rolling, it is easy and goes fast.

One end of the fence is wrapped around a huge cottonwood tree that serves as a post. Much of the bank has washed away, leaving the tree's roots exposed on one side, hanging over the bank like clawed witches' hands trying to grab the washed out earth. One day, when the rushing water carries away it's final support, the tree will fall into the creek. I cut the wires and unwrap two of them from around the tree. One is grown into the tree, cutting through the bark. As I lean over to undo it, the bank crumbles beneath my feet, and I have to grab the tree for support to avoid falling into the creek. I guess I'll leave that wire.

By the time I edge my way carefully around the tree and finish rolling the wire, Dad is loading up his wire rolls and old fence posts for firewood.

It's almost noon, and the sun is near the center of the sky, hot and yellow.

"After lunch, we'll come down and build that fence across the creek to keep your cows home," Dad says.

Across the creek from us is my house, and I can see my ten black cows standing in the corral, wanting to get out on grass instead of dry hay. The creek is not an effective barrier now that the water level is low, and they cross back and forth, getting into the neighbors' pastures.

"Good idea. Maybe Mom would like to come this time."

Building across the creek is a difficult job, and the fences have to be rebuilt each year, as flooding in the spring and ice jams during the winter tear out the wires and push out the posts. But it shouldn't take too long to build it today, with three of us working.

Ducks fly up from the creek, sprinkling water off their tails as they rise. Their green heads reflect the sunlight, and their feathers gleam. A heron flaps lazily away from his perch on a rock and comes to rest in the top of a cottonwood tree across the creek. He watches us for a moment, then flaps away, his long legs dangling.

On the other side of the creek is a fence built to the edge of a sandbar. On this side is a huge willow tree, bending over the creek. Dad wades out into the creek, wearing his waist-high irrigation boots, and I play the wire out as he carries it across. He wraps the wire around the post across the creek, and I wrap my end around the willow. As often as the fence will be replaced, the wires won't be around the tree long enough to hurt it. Dad hooks the wire stretchers to the wire so he can winch it tightly before stapling it to the post. Mom drives a steel post into the soft bank below the tree to hold the wires down so the cattle can't crawl under. She clips the wire as Dad gets it tight.

Three more wires are done the same way, making a sturdy four-wire fence. Dad takes a short piece of wire and wraps it around the top wire, weaving it through the other three and tying it under the water to a piece of junk metal, left over from an old car wreck. This will help hold the wires down. Now the cattle should stay home, in the right pasture.

Mom and Dad leave me at my house, and I pour myself a glass of tea before turning out my cows. They appreciate being loose, and the eight calves buck and kick, running with tails straight out behind them.

It's a beautiful afternoon, and not too hot. Taking a book, I go back outside to enjoy the rest of the day from my favorite seat on the haystack. From here I can see the blue mountains and Richard's car when he comes home from work.

FALL

IT FROSTED LAST NIGHT,
the first hard frost of the season. The big green leaves of the
squash and pumpkins are blackened,
withered now with the cold, looking
limp and dead. The big orange pumpkins stand out like golden basketballs
among the black leaves. The tomatoes
I had sense enough to pick last night
are sitting in a row on my windowsill
to ripen.

The trees up the creek are turning
from summer's deep green to
autumn's gold. The topmost leaves
caught the frost, making the leaves a
mixture of yellow and green. Soon the
leaves will be gone, floating to the
ground and drying to crispy brown
curls. Clouds are boiling up over the
mountains, hiding the top of Cloud
Peak and Black Tooth Mountain. The
wind smells metallic with storm.

The blackbirds are gathering up for
the trip south. Yesterday, coming
home from Buffalo, I saw a flock of
them on a newly cut field of straw.
Their glossy black feathers contrasted
strikingly with the golden stubble. As
I drove past, the flock rose off the
field like a black silk blanket being
shaken, then settled back down into
the yellow field. Today I hear above

me the hollow sound of wild geese, heading south. I scan the cloudy sky and finally see the V-shaped formation. The calls grow louder, and the V shuffles and reforms as the leaders change and reposition the flock.

I give up my nature watching and drive out to the ranch to see what Dad has planned for the day.

Dad has a full morning planned and is waiting for me when I drive in.

"Let's go up on the ridge in the creek pasture and gather up those empty barrels. I've got some full ones to put out for the steers."

The barrels are already in the pickup, half-barrels made from fifty gallon drums and filled with 200 pounds of a mineral supplement, thick with molasses. Cattle like it, and it provides vitamins and minerals that the cattle may be lacking on pasture alone.

"We may pick up some firewood too. There's a lot lying around that old corral," Dad says as I jump in the pickup.

"Has anyone called about the steers?" I'm always interested in our sales, because many of my cross-bred steers sell with the U Milliron herd. Cattle buyers call and offer money, and ranchers can either take it or hold out, hoping to get a better price.

"A guy called a couple days ago, but we're waiting for a better price." The market jumps up and down, and it is never easy to know when to sell. Buyers contract for the steers some months in advance of the shipping date, and the market could go up after we contract them or it could go down.

"How about the heifers?" Each year we sell the cull heifers, those that won't do well as brood cows.

"Haven't heard a thing on them."

96

The pickup groans as it climbs the steep road to the ridgetop, where we will gather the empty half-barrels and replace them with full ones. We scatter them on the ridges to encourage the steers to cover the entire pasture rather than eat out the grass close to the creek and waterholes. This way, they make better use of the pasture.

"When are we going to move the steers in this pasture?" I ask, throwing a barrel into the back end.

"Pretty soon," Dad says.

It doesn't take long to scatter the barrels, and then Dad drives to an old broken-down corral that we are slowly tearing down for the firewood in it. As we gather up the old posts, pulling out staples, nails, and wire to make for easier sawing, the wind comes up, blowing the clouds off the mountains and bringing the scent of rain. I feel one drop, then another, as the rain hits. Within minutes, the trees along the creek are shrouded with mist. The wet wood smells of decay.

My light jacket is soon soaked through. Dad throws one last post on the pickup, then gives it up. "Let's go. We're going to get wet."

The pickup feels warm and dry. "What do you mean, going to? Boy, this hit in a hurry."

"It might be slick getting out of here." Dad starts the engine, and the pickup bounces across the grass field to the dirt track that passes for a road. The rain has already turned the soft ground greasy, and the pickup slithered around as if it were driving through an oil slick. Looking behind us, the pickup tires have lifted the wet dirt off the road, leaving a dry track that is speckling with rain. These pasture roads are not graveled, so if a storm comes, it is important to get out fast, before the road becomes so muddy that the pickup can't maneuver it. Even a four-wheel-drive can get stuck in the thick gumbo mud, so unless it is of utmost importance, we don't travel the roads when they're muddy.

97

Today, we get to the gravel before the road gets any worse than slick. We leave some interesting tracks behind us. Back at the house, Mom's hot coffee feels good, and the warm house soon dries my damp clothes.

Sipping the coffee and listening to the rain pattering on the window, I think about the fall work that will begin soon. Shipping, always one of my favorite times since grade school, when I could skip school for a half day to help with the riding, will be coming up in a month or so. Weaning, shipping, and gathering require lots of horseback riding, one of my favorite ranch chores. Hunting season is just around the corner, and I look forward to stalking and downing a trophy deer and antelope.

"What's on your mind?" Mom asks.

"Fall work."

GATHERING

Gathering is an all-inclusive term used any time we take horses to gather up or bring in cattle. Gathering cattle, to move them from pasture to pasture, to bring in sick ones, or to get them ready to send to market, is done throughout the year.

Although we don't cover as much country with our gathers as they did in the early days when the country was open range, gathering is still a job for cowhands and good cow horses. Gathering usually means riding out before sunrise and often not getting home until after dark. It can involve wild chases across the countryside, or slow, dusty work in the drag. Gathering is one of the most enjoyable facets of the ranching life.

"Let's drive over into the association pasture and check the cattle," Mom says.

We try to check on them once in a while, to bring in cattle with cancer eye, or any with foot rot or other illnesses. Today, we also want to check the waterholes to make sure there is plenty of water and see that no cattle are bogged down in the thick mud.

The cattle are all hanging around the smaller reservoir in the pasture, the one that goes dry nearly every year. The reservoir is dried up to a tiny mudhole, and one cow has already fallen victim to the gooey mud. She has been dead for some time; her black belly is bloated up grotesquely, and her legs stick out stiffly.

"I wonder if she has a calf?" Mom says, and we walk back through the herd, looking for a calf that looks scroungier than the others, but all the calves look good.

"Maybe she was dry." It could be she didn't have a calf last spring.

"Maybe. We'd better saddle up this afternoon and push them down to the fish pond, where there's more water, before any more bog down," Mom says, referring to a larger pond about a half mile away. It always has water, and we used to plant trout in it for fishing, but they died out. For some reason, the cattle refuse to leave their favorite waterhole, even for a better one a short distance away. Unless we show them where the better water is, others might bog down and die, trying to drink from the dwindling pond. Occasionally, we can find them before they die and pull them out with a rope and a pickup, or a saddle horse. Otherwise, they will struggle until they die of exhaustion or starvation.

Walking back to the pickup, I look down into the draw near the reservoir again and see a Hereford bull standing on a small peninsula jutting out into the pond. He holds his right hind foot off the ground. The foot is swollen to almost twice it's normal size, probably a result of foot rot. He hops a little closer to the water and lowers his horned head for a drink. It is unlikely that he travels very far from that spot.

I nudge Mom. "Lame bull. I doubt if he can trail home." We are about three miles from Dad's and five miles from Bernard's.

"Maybe Bernard can come get him and load him in the trailer."

"They'll have to come and drag that cow out, or she'll foul any water that runs in there next spring."

Back at the house, we eat a quick lunch, then bring in the horse herd and saddle up for the ride. The weather is cooler now, with fall so near, or we probably wouldn't go out until later in the evening. During the midsummer months, afternoon riding is made miserable by the heat and the bloodsucking flies that torment the horses and cattle. Mike Lovato decides to join us and comes up leading Silver, the big Appaloosa we purchased last year.

Catawba is dancing impatiently after I mount, so I circle her around the driveway and then head down the road while Mom and Mike mount up. In a moment, I hear hoofbeats behind me, and we are on our way.

The cattle are still hanging around the dry reservoir, and the lame bull is lying down, resting his sore foot. Mom crosses the draw to gather the cattle on that hillside while Mike and I gather those on this side. One black bull breaks away and runs down into the draw, only to be stopped by the lame bull, who is irritable because of his lame foot and mad at being disturbed from his rest. The two bulls face each other and paw the ground. The lame bull, far from being de-terred by his bad foot, is still aggressive and shakes his head angrily. The black bull moves away, deciding not to challenge the older, larger bull. I watch the black bull until he joins

Mom's herd of cattle, then rein Catawba around to push up several cattle that are out of Mike's line of vision.

Once we get them gathered together, we ride behind them, pushing them toward the other pond, hoping they will water there instead of returning to this mudhole.

Coming up the hillside behind the cattle, I hear a buzzing sound, and my hands are full of panicked horse. Grabbing one rein, I spin her, as a horse cannot buck or run away in a spin. Catawba, obedient to the bit, spins, right on top of the rattlesnake again. She leaps into the air and lands running. I let her run until we catch up to the herd. We are both trembling when I pull her up. I hate to encounter snakes when I'm riding. I never know how a horse will react. Some horses don't seem to mind them, but others panic. I hope the snake didn't bite Catawba, but I doubt that it did. It was probably trying to get away from us just as fast as we were trying to get away from it. I smile, thinking about it from the snake's point of view.

"What happened?" Mike asks as I rejoin the herd.

"We had some fun with a rattlesnake. Catawba doesn't like snakes."

"Did she buck?"

"Nah, just jumped around a little."

The reservoir ahead is a deep, clear blue, looking like a giant blob of spilled blue paint. The grass around it is high and waving a little under the cattle's bellies. The hot summer sun has done it's work on the prairies, curing the once-green grass to a light tan. This cured grass is high in nutrients, putting fat on cattle and wildlife to help them withstand the cold winter months. The cattle bog down on the new feed, eating greedily. Why they didn't discover this waterhole before is something we don't understand. They can see the water from here and begin to graze in its general direction for a drink.

103

Several geese fly up off the pond, their calls echoing across the hills. The geese stay here all summer, a flock of about a hundred or so, occasionally even building nests and raising their young. Once we saw a mother goose and eight young ones waddling through the tall grass. They are beautiful birds, with long, slender necks and huge gray wings. The geese circle, waiting to land again, wanting us to go about our business so they can.

"This should be far enough, don't you think?" Mom turns Redwing's head homeward.

"If they can't see the water now, there's no hope for them anyway." We let the horses break into a trot. Catawba isn't limping, so I don't think she got bitten by the snake. She shies, her ears perked toward something in the grass. I think again of snakes, but it is only a gray and black badger, ambling away on his short furry legs. He ignores us, even when the three of us rein in to watch him. The long gray and white hair on his back falls over his sides, nearly touching the ground. It may be an early winter; the badger looks like he's making a winter coat.

Back at the ranch, Dad is waiting for us as we ride in. "Leave the horses we want in the corral. We have to gather steers tomorrow and bring them down to the creek pasture."

"What time are we going to leave?" Mom asks.

"We'll try to be up to the Perkins place to unload at about five." Dad turns to me. "You'll have to come out about four if you want breakfast."

We leave in three horses—Redwing, Gazelle, and Dynamite. The pasture they run in is large, so keeping them in makes things go faster in the morning. Otherwise, they could be at the far end of the pasture when we want them.

The air is nippy this morning, bringing the warning of winter. The wind is blowing from the west, off the Big Horn Mountains, bringing the smell of pine. Gazelle is prancing, full of nervous energy as I try to saddle him. The sky is still night-dark, with only a faint gray line on the horizon. Dad hitched up the trailer to the pickup last night, and he hands his horse's halter rope to me while he turns the rig around so we can load up. We will trailer the six miles up to where the steers are and bring them down the high ridge between here and the Perkins place.

By the time we get to the Perkins fence, it is daylight, but the sun has yet to make it's appearance. We are here at the agreed-upon time, but already Bernard and Linda are riding across the grass field toward several black spots that are steers. They have only a couple of miles to trailer, as compared to our six.

We mount up and turn our horses toward a deep draw. We will gather any steers that are in the draw, pushing them up along the fence line, across the grass field, and to a fence corner where we will hold them to sort off the ones we don't plan to take to market. Once we sort off the culls, we'll herd the rest down the ridge and put them in their new pasture.

There are several steers across the draw, and I head Gazelle toward them, leaving Dad and Mom to gather this side. The draw is steep, and I ride along the rim, looking for a good trail down. Finding a trail, I let Gazelle have his head, trusting him to pick the best footing. The draw bottom is full of long, deep swamp grass, growing over the ditchs and holes in the bottom. The other side of the draw is steep, and I have to ride down the draw until I can find a trail up.

An owl flies up in front of us, and Gazelle spooks a little. The owl is a great horned owl, common in this part of the country. Dad used to tell us kids that the draws were so deep the hoot owls would hoot in the daytime, thinking it was night. The draws aren't really that deep, but the sides are rugged and seem to close in on you when riding down them. Gazelle's ears twitch back and forth nervously; he doesn't

105

like draws. Maybe it's because his instincts warn him he can't run from danger as well down here.

Ahead is a trail, switchbacking up the hill. Gazelle sees it and heads toward it, pulling on the bit. Not knowing what kind of footing is underneath us, I hold him in and take the few feet of draw bottom slowly, rustling the swamp grass as we move through. The swamp grass hides a hole, and suddenly Gazelle's front end drops away from me. I get a close-up look at his ears, and the saddle horn digs into my belly. Several thoughts rush through my mind in that split second. Should I jump off and risk unbalancing Gazelle enough to pull him over on me, or should I sit tight, hoping he can get his footing despite my extra weight? I sit, and Gazelle finds his footing and leaps out of the hole, pulling himself up the steep trail in a series of jumps. Shaking, I push myself back into the saddle and turn my attention to my horse, but I can feel no difference in his bouncy stride. I hope he didn't strain his back or pull a muscle, but he seems fine.

Coming up over the rim of the draw, we are almost face-to-face with the wild-looking steers. Gazelle stops, surprised to see the cattle here. We came out of the draw just about right. Much lower, and we would have been behind them, pushing them back into the pasture, instead of back to the rest of the riders. I nudge Gazelle with my heels, and we move toward them. They stand ground for a moment, then wheel and dash off, heads high. They come to the fence line bordering the neighbors' pasture, then turn and dash hell-bent down the draw, kicking up dust. Gazelle and I follow at a more leisurely pace. The steers are going the right way; there is no need for us to race down the hillside.

The steers come to the draw bottom and turn up the draw instead of going across. Not exactly where I wanted them, but this will work out too. Going this way, they will join up with Bernard's herd, near the reservoir. Gazelle and I trot along behind, keeping the steers in sight but not pushing

106

them. They are going plenty fast. The draw makes a turn to
the right, and the steers follow it, heading to a spring that
Dad and Bernard developed a few years ago. The spring was
always there, but it needed the heavy black mud cleaned
from it so the water could flow freely. They also installed a
pipe to direct the water to a tank set in the hillside. Water
tanks and wells like this help to realize the full potential of
each pasture, as the cattle tend to feed near the waterholes
and leave other areas untouched.

The steers pile up around the water tank, drinking as if
they had just covered fifty miles of dry desert. I let them water, leaning on my saddle horn while Gazelle nips at the grass.
One turns to look at us, water dripping from his nose. When
they finish, I circle around to push them toward the reservoir. They trot away, full of water, most of the run out of
them. I can join up with Mom and Dad after all. They are
bringing up their herd along the tire tracks leading to the
pond.

"You got 'em," Dad says.

"Yeah, they had to stop for a drink at the spring."

"Poor things. If we didn't gather them once in awhile,
they'd die of thirst."

On a far hillside, we can see Bernard driving a bunch of
steers toward the reservoir. Linda must be down in the other
draw, the one that runs below the reservoir dike. "Cynthy,
you and your Mom ride down and see if Linda needs help.
I'll ride over and help Bernard." We leave our herd by the
reservoir and trot along the edge of the draw, looking for
steers and riders. Below us, we see a herd of steers, meander-
ing up the draw toward the reservoir. Across the draw Linda
is chasing a bunch of runaways, trying to convince them to
go down in the draw with the others.

Finding a trail down, we drop into the draw, behind the
steers. I start up the other side to help Linda, but she has

107

them turned, and I see one, than another, slip and slide down the trail.

The steers rejoin our herd, and Linda rides along the rim above us to collect any on the hillsides and to be up out of the draw in case any break away from us. Two think about it, and they try to break off and run up a branch of the draw, but Gazelle and I head them back to the herd.

The draw bottom contains several dead cottonwood trees, their branches and trunks white and bleached, like sunbleached bones. Some of the trees are still standing, and the bark is shiny and smooth from generations of cattle rubbing and scratching itchy hides on the bark. I wonder what this valley looked like when the trees were alive, with warm green leaves covering the skeletal branches. It was probably pretty then, and deer and cattle could lie beneath the trees, shaded from the hot summer sun. Now the trees will soon fall and be ground to pulp under the feet of the cattle and the gradual wear of decay.

Reaching the dike, we push the steers up out of the draw to join those on the hillside. I take a rough count of the steers and come up with sixty-two. We need about two hundred. "We'll have to find a few more," I tell Mom. "There's a few back on the grass field below the trailer, but not enough to make two hundred."

"I guess we'll find them," Mom says. We wait, watching the steers and the sun shining off the ripples of the pond. Perkins, the man who owned this land before my grandfather bought it, once drowned a team of horses in this pond. I forget what he was doing, but the horses tangled in the harness, and he didn't get them out in time. I've always wondered if the skeltons are still there under the black, stagnant-smelling mud.

"Here comes your Dad and Bernard," Mom says. The steers are trailing over the skyline, and Linda is sitting on her horse below them making sure none run down the draw we just came up. The steers are easy to count coming over the ridge, and I come up with forty.

"So far, we have one hundred."

Bunching the steers together, we move them toward the trailers, picking up grazing steers as we go. Bunched together, the herd looks smaller than it is, but we have covered the entire pasture, so unless some are out of the pasture, we should have all of them. Bernard rides ahead, opening the gate between this pasture and the one we have to herd them through to get them home.

"I thought we were going to sort them." I ride up alongside Dad.

"We decided to take them down to the corral and sort them, then truck off the extras."

I ride around the herd, pushing them up and keeping them moving toward the gate. The steers, unused to the gate being open, begin to mill around, trying to turn away from the fence. The riders keep pushing them from all sides, steadily, but not too fast. We don't want to crowd them through the wire fence. Once one sees the open gate and goes through, the rest follow, stringing through like a ribbon of cattle. Bernard is waiting on the other side of the gate, counting the steers as they file through. Finishing the count, Bernard falls in place near the leaders to keep the front end of the herd moving in the right direction. Dad rides through the gate and takes his place on the other side of the lead, making sure they don't go down in the draw, pushing them toward the high ridge.

The steers trot out eagerly, wanting to go to new pastures. Mom, Linda, and I ride in the drag, keeping the slower ones pushed up. The ridge narrows, so Dad drops back with us, and Bernard rides point. The steers seldom give trouble going down the ridge, as the steep sides discourage most of them from trying to get away. We used to drive them down

109

the draw, but since Bernard built the pickup road down the ridge, this works better.

I've heard that Granddad once asked a man to build a road down this ridge, but the man took a look at the large rock outcroppings along the top and said a road couldn't be built. Bernard didn't know about the rocks and built the road.

By 10:00 A.M. we are nearly home. The steers boil down the ridge along the road, where we want them to go. But instead of turning to the right, some break left at the bottom of the hill, bucking and kicking across the grass field. Bernard, cussing, leaps his horse after them, but the steers refuse to go back, circling around behind his horse. Dad gallops Dynamite up to help him, and together they get the steers turned and headed home. The rest of the herd follows them, stringing along toward the draw.

The leaders still want to run, and they run down the draw, up the other side, and stop for a minute at the edge of the plowed field, which is ready for seeding in wheatgrass. Bernard, Linda, and I gallop up to keep them from going the wrong way. Gazelle stumbles a little as he hits the lumpy, plowed ground but keeps going. Defeated, the steers turn and head toward the corrals for sorting and then to be moved to another pasture to await shipping day.

SHIPPING DAY

During the days of the trail drives from Texas to the northern railheads, the day when the drovers finally arrived in town was a day for celebration. It meant payday, a time of compensation for discomfort endured and dangers faced. It meant women, saloons, and the excitement of town. Many cowhands, bored with life on 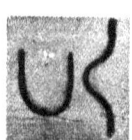 *the trail, blew off steam when they hit town, and many of the more staid elements of the towns wanted the drives stopped. During the 1870s, Texas fever began wiping out domestic cattle, so legislation was enacted to keep the Longhorns off the Kansas ranges. These factors, along with the trend toward meatier cattle, caused the decline of the trail era.*

Shipping day is still a day for collecting money for the steers, but the drives to the shipping point are shorter, and cattle are often loaded on trucks rather than trains. Sometimes cattle are trucked to the sale barns in hope of getting a better price.

The alarm buzzes at 4:00 A.M., knocking aside a dream that I can't remember now. The kitten jumps off the bed, and I can hear him running through the house, knowing I will feed him. Today is shipping day, the day we drive the cull heifers to the stockyards in Clearmont for delivery to the buyer who contracted them earlier in the year. Next week, we will ship the two-year-old steers.

I trip over Fizz Bomb, who is meowing for his breakfast. I feed him, then pull on my boots, overshoes, and coat for the chilly morning ride. The morning is still black, and the air is cold. The pickup heats up slowly, but by the time I reach Dad's it is warm and cozy. I almost hate to get out into the cold, but I know that breakfast is waiting inside.

Breakfast is ready, with floury biscuits, bacon, and fresh ranch eggs. Water is boiling on the coal stove for hot tea. The kitchen is warm and golden after the cold morning.

"Is Dean going to help?" I ask Dad. Dean usually helps.

"I saw him go by just a minute ago. I guess he'll eat with Bernard."

The morning is still dark when we finish breakfast and untangle bridles to catch the horses. Gazelle lets me walk up to him, but he shies away when I try to catch him. After two complete circles around the corral to show me that he isn't going to give in easily, Gazelle stops and lets me bridle him.

The garage where we keep the saddles and horse equipment is dimly lit—one of the big fluorescent bulbs in the light fixture is burned out—and saddles and tiedowns are hard to find. The horses stand patiently, awaiting the blankets and saddles, resigned to being our servants for another day.

My cinch is too long. Someone has been riding my saddle on a big horse. I have to take up the slack three notches to fit Gazelle's tiny girth.

"Who's been riding my saddle?"

"Mike and Linda went out yesterday. Linda rode your saddle on Dynamite," Mom explains.

"No wonder." I look at Dynamite, Dad's tall chestnut, standing about sixteen hands. Gazelle was a stallion until he was three years old, and we raised a few colts from him. Dynamite is his son, but he inherited few of the Arabian characteristics.

The sky is just getting gray in the east by the time we mount up and ride to the pasture where the heifers have been summering. The hills and the skyline are the only sure things in this early morning land of shadows. "We can't even see a cow yet," I mutter, thinking of the extra half hour I could have spent dreaming.

Mom, hearing me, agrees. "I didn't think there was any sense getting up until five thirty."

"Oh well, maybe we can find some cows."

Dad has left us farther back, working down the draw bottom, trying to spook the heifers out of the brushy bottomlands. Mom and I climb our horses to the top of the ridge. From here we will be able to see off both sides when it grows light enough to see.

Slowly the daylight is creeping up, turning the cardboard-shadow hills into three-dimensional shapes of rocks and washouts. The valleys and sage begin to take shape below us. We ride along the skyline, able to see objects in the increasing light.

We see a rider below us on the meadow, but no cattle on either side of the ridge. The rider disappears from sight down into the draw. Mom and I nudge our horses into a trot, then a lope, wanting to catch up with the rest of the riders. There are no cattle here, so the bulk of them must be in the draw. The slope is steep as we go off the ridge, and the horses slip and slide on the loose dirt.

114

The heifers are coming up out of the draw on the far side; the other riders must be behind them. Mom and I keep the horses at a steady pace until we catch up and fall in behind the herd. Sheila Betz and Dean are with this herd, and Dad, Linda Betz, and Bernard are trying to round up a herd of heifers that are running down the draw. The runaways find a trail out of the draw and gallop up it, running flat out as they hit the meadow. Dad, Bernard, and Linda swing in a wide circle, galloping to head them.

Our herd stops, feeding on the tall grass on the hillside. We wait, holding them just enough to make sure they don't scatter off. From our location we watch the drama of cowhands versus cattle on the flat across from us. The heifers don't want to turn, but finally, outrun by the faster horses, they wheel and plunge down into the draw again, swirling through the greasewood and spooking our herd as they run up the hill. The cattle leap from a standstill into a run, and I jump Gazelle out to head them. They run as far as the fence, then stop and turn back toward the gate.

Seeing that the heifers are under control, Bernard gallops up and opens the gate, waiting on the other side to turn the cattle down the gravel road that they will follow to the next pasture.

Bernard rides ahead of the heifers to give them a leader and to run off any of the two-year-old steers that might get in our way in the creek pasture. We trail them down the country road a ways, blocking the movement of one pickup, whose driver eases through the herd then waves as he passes us. Bernard opens the gate into the creek pasture, and the heifers string through, looking like a brown, black, and yellow snake, winding and twisting down the road. The cattle are a mixed herd, with Herefords, black baldies, and Charolais crosses.

Dad rides up beside me. "How much do you think they'll weigh?"

Each year we make a small wager on the weight of the cattle, and sometimes I'm right. "About 650 pounds," I take a guess, looking over the herd. Several are good, big heifers, but many are smaller, and they lower the average.

"I'll say 625." Dad likes to guess them low. If they weigh out heavier, he doesn't mind losing the bet.

Trotting back to where Mom is riding drag, I ask, "How about fifty cents on how much they'll weigh? I said 650, Dad says 625."

Mom guesses light. "Six-twenty. Some of them aren't very big."

The dust boils up from the dry road. We let the heifers move slowly, not running them unless we're trying to turn back some runaways. Moving them slowly keeps them from losing weight, and they are easier to handle. We have to be at the stockyards by nine, but we still have two hours to get there. We should be there about on time, barring trouble at the creek or railroad bridge, the two worst spots on the drive.

The lead heifers reach the creek and stop to tank up on the rushing water. The rest crowd up, shoving their noses into the water. The riders wait, letting them water, knowing the buyer will take a 3 percent shrink off the price to allow for this. When the heifers begin to move away from the water, we push them along the creek, through the meadow we poisoned spurge in last summer, to the crossing.

Dad and Bernard have been at work constructing a partial fence from the high, steep bank out into the creek. The cattle usually won't try to climb the bank, which is about twenty feet of loose dirt, so with the fence and the bank, there is only one way for them to go—into the creek.

The riders close in behind them, crowding the heifers, yelling and whooping to scare them in. The heifers, unused to running water, balk and mill around, not wanting to cross, not wanting to face the horsemen. Heads on red haunches,

116

they look like a living whirlpool of cattle. One tries to claw her way up the steep bank but falls back into the herd. One darts between Linda and Sheila, and two others follow her lead. They run back across the meadow, and Gazelle and I wheel to head them, galloping across the meadow, up the road, and down into the gravel pit. Sheila follows, and as I swing around in front of them, she is there, catching them as they try to break around me again. They give up and run back to the herd, jostling in among the other heifers and forcing one into the creek. She sniffs the water, then tentatively takes first one step, then another. Soon she is belly-deep in water, and the others, seeing they have a leader, follow. Slowly, the herd crosses the creek, dripping as they climb up the bank on the far side. Dad and Bernard ride on either side to keep them moving.

The cattle are crossing well, so with no need to hurry, I let Gazelle pick his way across the slick, mossy rocks slowly. In one place the water is deep enough to touch my stirrup, and some splashes up on my pants leg. Gazelle tugs at the reins, so I let him drink, then he splashes across the creek and up the bank.

The lead cattle are already well ahead of us, crossing the slough between here and the highway fence. Dad and Bernard took down the fence last night so the heifers would have a clear shot at the highway crossing. This is the old highway, so most of the traffic is local farmers and ranchers. There are few cars out this morning, so there is little worry about anyone hitting a cow. Once across the highway, we will drive them up the meadow and under the railroad bridge to avoid crossing the railroad tracks as we used to do.

One time, several years ago, a train came as we were almost ready to cross the tracks. The train schedules are unpredictable, and we were lucky that we didn't have the steers halfway across before the train came, whistle screaming. The steers bolted back across the highway and through the wire fence on the other side. We didn't lose too many, and no one was injured, but it slowed us down. Now we go under the bridge, but we would still have trouble if a train came.

The grass on the meadow is almost belly deep on the heifers, and they graze eagerly, liking the irrigated grass after the dry pasturelands. A group of pheasants fly up in front of them and they shy, almost in unison. The leaders stop suddenly as they hit a strip of marshy ground. Then they hesitantly go across.

Ahead is the railroad bridge, crossing a dry roadbed. The heifers began to mill around, not liking the shadow under the bridge or the arch above them. The riders do little except circle the herd, keeping the rebels from dashing away, back to the meadow. Bernard rides into the herd, separating two or three and urging them under. Once they go, the rest follow. Dean rides across the tracks to turn the cattle toward the stockyards, now only a quarter mile away.

The big cattle trucks are already waiting for their load, and the pickups near the scale house tell us that the brand inspector and the cattle buyer are there as well. We turn the cattle through the gate into the corrals with no trouble and dismount, tying the horses to the long plank wing off the corrals. Now it's time for footwork, running the heifers past the brand inspector so he can check the brands and separating bunches of twenty-four off to run across the scale for the average.

The heifers average out at 640 pounds, a little lighter than I guessed, but I was still the closest.

"Not bad," Dad says.

"Pretty good heifers," I agree.

The heifers are shipped, and the money is collected. Today we have to ship out the big two-year-old steers. We will also bring them across the creek and into the stockyards. The steers have been pastured here on the creek since August, so they should be accustomed to the water.

Dad, Mom, and I ride from Dad's house through the willow grove and into the back side of the pasture. Several steers are lying near the water tank, put in here two years ago to get maximum use out of the pasture. The steers look disgusted with us for waking them this early, and they get to their feet slowly. They are huge animals, weighing around a thousand pounds apiece.

"These are good big ones," Mom comments.

"Ought to weigh out well," Dad says, swinging back on Dynamite after opening and closing the gate. We ride up to the steers, and they watch us, not wanting to move unless necessary. Mom and I push them up out of the draw, and Dad urges Dynamite up the other side. He will check the rough back country for steers while Mom and I trail these toward the creek, picking up any along the way. We find four more on the grass flat and six more grazing in a draw off the ridge. The trail is steep up the ridgetop, and the steers grunt and heave going up.

The ridge is windy, but the sun is also up here, touching everything with gold light. Suddenly, Catawba stops and shifts into reverse so fast I have to fight with myself to get back into the saddle. I calm her, wondering what spooked her.

Mom looks in the sage ahead of us and laughs. "A snake skin."

I can see the skin as Catawba jumps past the sagebrush. Some snake has used this brush to shed his skin. "She hasn't gotten over her rattlesnake scare yet," I say, patting her neck to show I don't really mind. She nods her head, mane bouncing.

Below us and to our left are several steers, and I leave Mom following the herd on the ridge while I turn Catawba down the hill. The hillside is steep, and loose sand rolls out from under her hooves, making her bounce to keep her footing. I let her have her head, trusting her to take us to the bot-

119

tom safely. The slope flattens out, and we are on the leveler ground. Catawba whinnies back to Redwing, who answers her, and far away I hear Dynamite, whinnying lonesomely. Catawba shakes her head as I turn her after the steers, but she quits her horse talk and settles down to business.

The steers, ambitious in the cool morning, turn tail and run when they see us, galloping clumsily toward the small waterhole, which is still holding a little muddy-looking water. Rather than turn them back up the ridge, I follow them. As long as they keep going in the general direction of the creek, that's all that matters. Mom's herd will come off the ridge soon, and she will join up with us.

The steers bunch up at the pond. They water, then string out in a long line toward the creek. Mom's herd boils off the ridge and joins the ones I picked up.

"It looks like they'll go," Mom says. "Lets ride up over the ridge and check that next pond."

On the skyline of the farthest ridge in the pasture I see a rider coming this way. It's probably Dad, checking the other side of the ridge along the neighbors' fence. In a minute he disappears from sight. Around the pond are eighteen steers, so we round them up and head them back to join with our herd.

"Most of the steers must be on the creek." I noticed that the rider on the skyline wasn't trailing anything, and even with the 18 we just gathered, our herd won't number over 50. There should be around 160 steers in the pasture.

"Maybe they're licking the tubs," Mom adds. "Getting fat."

"These look pretty fat already. Look at that one." A tall, heavy black baldy steer has stopped to look at us, wondering if he really has to move. He should weigh around 1200 pounds.

"Most of them look pretty good this year," Mom says.

120

Most of the steers are around the creek, lying under the trees and licking at the molasses mixture in the tubs. We drop our herd off and ride back up the road to see if the others we collected are still trailing along. They are still coming, but slowly, so we drop into the draw behind them to keep them moving along. Off to the east we see another herd. It must be Linda and Sheila trailing the steers from the wheat-grass field near the county road. It looks like there are about seventy animals.

We wait near the tubs and exchange greetings with Linda and Sheila as they ride up. "How many do we have?" Linda asks.

"We had about seventy or so. How many were in your herd?"

"Sixty-five. We're short some."

"Maybe Wallace and Bernard will find some. I hope none got out," Mom says.

Behind us, I see another herd coming, and two riders behind it. There should be enough now to make the count. Gathering the steers together, we push them toward the creek. Used to the water, they dive right in, stopping to drink as they splash across.

The steers go well until we come to the highway. Then they balk and refuse to step on the pavement. The riders push them, and finally one goes, and the rest, except for four, follow. Most of the riders follow the main herd, but Dad and Bernard stay behind to see if the four contrary ones will cross. One jumps through the fence into my pasture and runs back down to the creek and across, going back to the hills. The others still show no sign of crossing, so Bernard shakes out his rope and ropes one, dragging it across. Feet set, the steer fights the head rope, but there is little he can do. He could plow furrows if the road were soft, instead of paved. Across the road, Bernard takes the rope off, and the steer runs to join the herd. The other two give up and cross.

121

"What about the one that got away?" I ask Bernard as he rides up.

"Maybe we'll butcher him," Bernard grins.

The steers travel through the meadow at a trot, then stop as they are confronted by the railroad bridge. They mill, and two dive past the riders and scramble up the steep shale bank and onto the railroad. Dean rides up and pushes them back down with the herd. It takes awhile, but they go under, and the rest is easy.

Today, despite the trouble on the highway, we are early, and the trucks haven't yet shown up. We corral the steers and dismount, waiting for the trucks and the brand inspector.

"I could go for a beer," Dad says. "Cynthy, why don't you and your mom ride over and get some?"

Shipping, like branding, is a time of beer drinking. Even though it is only a little after 8 A.M., we have been up for four hours, and a beer tastes good after a long ride. The bars, two of them, are just across the tracks and the highway. Dad gives me a ten dollar bill, and Mom and I swing back into our saddles.

"How are we going to carry beer?" Mom asks.

I hear an eager whinny behind us and turn in my saddle to see Dynamite, reins trailing, galloping up. He hates to be left alone, and Dad never ties him tightly.

I reach down and grab the trailing reins to lead him along. "We'll make Dynamite a beer packing horse."

The bar is nearly empty, but I take some kidding from an old friend. "You must plan to buy a lot of beer. I see you've got a packhorse."

"We're mighty dry after that long trail," I try to drawl.

They all laugh as I pay and collect the two sixpacks of beer and one of pop.

122

I wrap the drinks in Dad's coat and tie it to Dynamite's saddle. An evil thought crosses my mind. "I wonder if they're in a hurry. We could trot all the way."

"We'd better not," Mom laughs. We walk the horses slowly.

The trucks are waiting when we get back, but the vet and brand inspector haven't shown up. We used to load cattle out on freight cars, and we'd have to wait until noon for the train. Afterwards, the buyer would treat us to lunch at the Red Arrow cafe. It made a nice touch for the end of the morning's work. Now we are usually done by eleven o'clock.

We have time for one can of beer before the vet drives in, followed by the brand inspector. Now we can get a clean bill of health on them, check for any neighbor's strays, and find out how many of each of our three brands there are. Most are company, or U Milliron, cattle, but Mom and I and my sister have a few wearing the L Milliron brand, and Bernard has a few P Bars.

Then we will weigh them and collect our money.

WEANING

Weaning usually happens in late October or during November. The calves are around six months old. Some ranchers sell calves at this time as well.

Since it happens so late in the year, weaning is usually a cold, miserable job, and we often encounter snow. It gives us an appreciation of hot coffee and warm fires. During this time we also have the vet down to bangs vaccinate the young heifers to protect against brucellosis, a contagious disease.

Weaning gives the cows a chance to gain strength again before having to convert too much energy to the growing calf inside them. Most ranchers wean the calves off the young heifers earlier, to allow for better growth in the young heifers. The weaned calves are watched closely for illness and fed well over the winter so they will reach the desired weight by spring.

The wind is blowing on the ridges as we unload the horses to start the drive. The clouds hang low, heavy with snow.

"We never make this drive down country without getting wet," I mutter, warming Catawba's bit in my gloved hands. "Every year, it storms."

"You got to expect snow in November," Dad says, snapping Dynamite's tiedown to the ring on the cinch.

"Are Bernard and Linda already gathering?" Mom asks. I glance across the wheatgrass field, trying to see if there are any riders.

"They unloaded across the hill. They'll gather everything on the reservoir and push them up over the ridge. We'll gather this side."

Catawba skitters and jumps as I mount, excited by the storm in the air. I have a feeling this is going to be a long, cold ride. Several cows and calves are huddled under the shelter of some chokecherry bushes in a shallow draw. I ride above them and yell, not wanting to ride through the brushy tangle unless necessary. The cattle, jittery from the wind and cold, spook and run out of the draw, crackling branches and bucking up the hillside.

The cattle turn and run the wrong way, and I kick Catawba into a gallop to head them. Catawba, liking the sport of chasing cows, leaps forward. A ditch appears ahead of us, and she takes it in a smooth leap. I wish I remembered enough of my jumping lessons to be more prepared for it, but I feel I do rather well and enjoy the floating feeling. Jumping would be fun, but I sold my English saddle. Someday, I may buy another one and take up jumping again, but for now I'll stick to my stock saddle, which is much more practical for stock work, with the high pommel and cantle to help balance the rider as the horse turns after stock.

The cows and calves turn and head up a faint trail that leads up the ridge, then turns right along the ridgetop. We used to drive the cattle down the draw, but the ridge works better, and the cattle are less likely to try to get away from the steep sides. One year a blizzard caught us in the draw, and the wind blew the snow up it as if it were a wind tunnel, covering the cattle and horses with thick, wet flakes and making it hard to distinguish animals in the storm. I hope it doesn't snow this year, as the high, unprotected ridge will be colder than the draw.

Almost as if nature could read my thoughts, the wind comes up stronger, and I feel two or three wet flakes of snow melt on my face. "It's going to storm," I tell Catawba, pulling her around to help Dad and Mom, pushing up several cattle to join my small herd. "At times like this I wish we were still driving them down the draw. It's more sheltered from the wind."

"This is faster, though," Mom says. "We'll get done quicker."

I watch the grass bend before the wind. To the west the Big Horn Mountains are wrapped in downy gray clouds. I'm glad the wind is at my back, instead of coming into my face. It's warm this way, and the cattle move better, as it is in their nature to drift in front of a storm, turning their tails to the wind and snow.

Cattle start to head up the ridge, joining our herd. From below I hear Bernard and Linda yelling at them to push them along. Mom, Dad, and I rein in our horses and wait until first Linda, then Bernard come up the ridge, their horses steaming from the sweat on their necks. Linda falls in beside me, and Bernard rides along the side of the ridge.

"Sheila must be in school today," I comment, noticing that my young cousin isn't along on this drive.

126

"We were going to keep her out, but she had a test to-day, so we thought she'd better go." Linda's voice is soft, slightly drawling.

I laugh knowing that Sheila, like me when I was younger, would rather be riding with us in the cold, biting wind than sitting in a warm schoolroom, thinking about the ride. "I'll bet she'd rather be here, wouldn't she?"

"Yeah, she would."

The sun comes through the cloudcover, white and weak. The clouds make a halo around it, making it look bigger than normal, like a huge, round cloud.

Some of the cattle break down a steep trail off the ridge, going around the side of a small hill and breaking my imaginings. Dad gallops off to head them, his horse slipping dangerously on the steep, sandy hillside. In a minute they disappear around the hill, going after the cattle. Bernard has disappeared too, and I see him ahead of us, opening the gate and standing beside it to make sure the cattle don't miss the opening and walk around it. Dad comes back with the runaways, and they trail through the gate, followed by the rest of the herd.

I feel a fever blister starting on my lip. The constant exposure to wind and dry cold cracks my lips and encourages the fever blisters. It hurts, but I left my medicine in my other coat. I'll have to wait until I get home.

The snowstorm has started. The white flakes whirl around the herd and make the valleys below us look fuzzy. We aren't far from home now, so we won't have to ride too long in the wet snow. The cattle drop off the ridge along the road and turn and trot in the right direction, toward the corrals. It is only about a mile home now, and then the real work begins.

The cattle go into the corral with no trouble, and now it is time for the footwork. We have a full day ahead of us yet. We have to run each cow into the squeeze chute to adminis-

127

ter Spot-On, a grub control medication that has to be poured on the cattle's backs. We will also sort the calves from the cows and put the grub control medicine on them as well.

Bernard dismounts and shuts the gate behind the herd. Dad dismounts and gives me Dynamite's reins. "Take him up and unsaddle him, will you?"

Mom rides over with me, to check on dinner. Dynamite gives the impression of a horse on his last legs as he hangs his big head to his knees. I'd feel sorry for him, but I know better. As soon as I turn them out, he gallops away, bucking and kicking in joy to be done for the day.

"Need any help with dinner?"

"No. I've got a turkey in the oven. You'd better go back down and help out in the corral."

That's fine with me. I'd rather be working livestock than setting a table or cooking.

Dad, Bernard, and Linda are already at work. Several cows and calves have been run up in the long, narrow alley for sorting. Dad is handling the big gate near the top of the alley, letting the calves run around behind him into the round corral and letting the cows go out the gate into the bigger corral. My job is helping Bernard and Linda push the cattle up the alley so the calves can be sorted off at the gate. It takes about an hour to separate the cows and calves, and the air is filled with the noisy bawling of calves wanting their mothers, and cows answering. In a few days, the calves will forget and learn to be grownup cattle. But now they are lonely and frightened.

The calves are shut in the round corral, waiting for their turn through the squeeze chute. The cows are run from the big corral into the alley again so we can run them into the squeeze. Dad and Linda push the cattle down the alley and into the smaller pen near the squeeze. They can't all fit, so we are satisfied to put in twenty at a time. From the smaller holding pen, a narrow alley, wide enough for one cow, opens

128

into the squeeze chute. Dad and Linda, yelling and thumping on the cattle with short lengths of plastic pipe, spook three of them into the alley, closing the gate behind them.

Bernard, ready with the Spot-On, opens the sliding gate between the alley and the squeeze. I am operating the head catch, which is open enough now for the cow to stick her head through, but not wide enough to allow the shoulders out. Seeing the opening, the cow runs into the chute, and as her head goes through the opening, I quickly pull on the rope that closes the head catch. The cow bucks and struggles but is held securely as Bernard squirts on the Spot-On. To make the work go faster, Bernard treats the other cows in the alley, then nods to me to let them out. I hit the release lever with the heel of my hand, opening the head catch and letting the cows jump out.

Bernard comes over so I can hear him above the bawling cattle. "Don't catch them. Just shut the head gate, and we'll doctor all of them in the alley. Then you can turn them out."

I watch Bernard, and he nods to me as he finishes so I can open the head gate and let the cows out. My arm begins to tire from pulling the rope, and my hand hurts where I have to hit the release lever. The cattle herd behind me is increasing slowly, but there are still a lot of cattle left to doctor.

I hit the catch to let a cow out, and the gate jams. I see the problem—the cow in the chute has tried to push her way out around the sides of the head gate and is now caught between the bars of the head gate and the chute. I pull the head gate shut again, but she still can't get out. She tries to go forward instead of backing up.

"Trouble," I yell to Bernard, and he and Dad come up to help, trying to push the cow's wildly lunging head back into the chute. The cow struggles, jumping and kicking, and for a moment it seems that she will tear the whole structure

129

to pieces before finally pulling her head back. Bernard opens the head catch and lets her go.

"Cynthy, use the back gate, and we'll doctor them in the alley," Bernard says, meaning the sliding gate at the other end of the chute. We can turn them out the small gate alongside the alley and not even have to use the chute. It will need a few repairs after the damage the cow did, but it would still work if we really needed it. Squeeze chutes are probably one of the best things ever invented for handling cattle easily and safely.

Finally, the last cow is doctored. Mom comes down to let us know that dinner is ready, so we decide to eat before working with the calves. Then we will follow the same procedure we did with the cows, except we will also load them in trucks for the trip to Bernard's. For a week or so, they will stay there, forgetting their mothers and learning to eat cattle cake. Then we will truck them to our place near Buffalo, where they will live for the winter.

Tomorrow, we will need these corrals empty for separating and doctoring a new bunch of cows and calves—we'll bring in the ones that are being run on shares with Dean Floate.

Today is warmer than yesterday, and the snow quit last night, leaving only a skift of snow on the ground. Dad and I will ride from his house, and Bernard and Dean will trailer the horses and start at the other end of Dean's pasture. The pasture is small and the cattle are easy to gather. Within an hour's time we have them strung out along the gravel road, heading to Dad's house. The road is fenced on both sides, and Dean and Bernard ride ahead to open corral gates and be at the corral to keep the cattle from going past. Dad and I trot easily behind the cattle, keeping them moving.

Several cows climb the steep road bank and walk along the fence, stopping to grab bites of grass here and there. To keep them moved up, I jump Catawba up the bank to follow them along the fence line.

The trail follows the fence closely, and as I ride along, a barb catches my pant leg. I try to free my leg, but the barb is stuck too deep. Catawba, sensing something is wrong, jumps sideways. The wire pulls away from the fence and twangs, ripping my jeans and hitting Catawba in the haunch. Catawba, green broke and scared, leaps forward and comes down stiff legged and bucking. Off balance from leaning down to free my leg, I am unprepared for the buck. I try to regain my balance, but suddenly Catawba's head disappeares as she drops off the steep road bank, bucking as she hits the bottom. The combination of the bucking and the downward plunge is unbalancing, and I feel myself flying through the air, only to come to a jarring halt on the hard-packed gravel road.

For a long moment I can't breathe. It feels like a heavy weight is pressing down on my chest, and no air can get into my lungs. I gasp, trying to breathe. Getting my breath, my right side hurts with the movement. I hope I haven't broken any ribs.

I see Dad hovering over me, looking worried. "You okay?"

"I think so. Just knocked the wind out of me. I don't think I'm hurt."

"I'll go back and get the pickup. Just stay here. Did you hurt your back?" I know he's remembering a friend of ours who broke her back when a horse bucked her off. Now she's paralyzed from the waist down.

"I think I can ride in a minute." I push myself up with my left hand and feel okay, except for the pain in my right shoulder. I probably pulled some muscles. Dad helps me stand and then catches Catawba for me. Surprisingly, she didn't run home, which is only a quarter mile away. She is standing not far away, trembling a little, waiting for me. I

131

pick up her reins, pet her a little, and soothe her with words. I want to get back on, as a horse that finds out bucking a person off leads to getting out of being ridden might try again.

Catawba stands to be mounted, and I reach for the saddle horn, but my right arm won't reach that high. The pain starts at my shoulder and goes down my arm. I try again and slowly reach the horn. My arm feels numb. I pull myself lightly into the saddle, and a feeling of faintness comes over me as I settle into the seat. I grit my teeth, fighting it, and it passes. I squeeze my knees to signal Catawba to move out. As long as I don't try to use my right arm, the shoulder isn't too painful, but bad enough.

"I think I pulled some muscles in my shoulder. I guess you guys can corral them alright if I quit at the house."

Dad nods. "We can get them. Go ahead."

I have more trouble getting off than I did getting on, and I know I won't be able to unsaddle Catawba by myself. Mom didn't come on this ride, and she is in the house. I lead Catawba up to the patio and yell for Mom to come help me. She takes one look at me and orders me into the house to lie down while she takes my horse.

When Mom comes back, she calls the doctor despite my protests that no bones are broken. I don't think I could have mounted again if I had broken anything. Still, she is determined to make sure. I take six aspirins to help the pain, a fact that will scandalize the doctor's nurse. They dull the pain a little, but now that the shock has worn off, my shoulder hurts, especially when Mom hits the bumps in the highway. The thirty miles to Buffalo seems long.

The X-rays reveal a broken collarbone, proving me wrong. I guess it was a good thing I came in, after all. The doctor gives me a brace to help hold the collarbone in place while it's healing, as they are difficult to set. Mom called Richard from home before we left, and he and my cousin Mary

132

Lou, who is car pooling to work with him, walk in as the nurse gives me some codeine tablets for pain.

"I've told you to quit riding them broncs," Mary Lou kids.

"I like the excitement," I tell her.

My shoulder hurts more now than it did when I fell off, but I don't blame my horse. She was scared and didn't really know what to do. She'll get a vacation for a while. No riding for six weeks, until my collarbone heals.

I'm just lucky not to have been more badly hurt.

"You want some supper?" Rich asks.

"I'm not sure I can eat, but I would like an iced tea."

We stop at Taco John's, and I order a burrito. Food and iced tea help settle my stomach.

"So the poor kid broke her collarbone?" Rich says. He's never broken a bone in his life, and this is the first time I have.

"That's what happens to bronc riders."

"YOU WANT TO RIDE out and gather cedar greens?" Mom asks, as we sit sipping hot tea in front of the fireplace. My collarbone is healed now; I took the brace off last week. This is a slow time of year—fall work, weaning, and shipping are over, and feeding usually does not begin until the first week in January. A horseback ride across the snowy landscape would be fun.

"Sure, where are we going?" There are several cedar groves around the ranch, and each year Mom cuts some to give the house a Christmasy look. The cedar perfumes the house with a spicy, green fragrance, and after Christmas it smells nice burning in the fireplace. Christmas is a week away. Usually Mom gathers cedar earlier, but this is the first day we've had that the temperature hasn't been below zero.

The sun is shining, turning the snow a glaring silver, washing out everything but the brilliant blue sky. It isn't really warm; the thermometer reads a chilly twenty degrees above zero, but it is better than the twenty degrees below zero we have been experiencing. Last year, during the extreme cold, Richard went out to bring

in a Christmas tree, and it was so cold the needles froze and fell off before we could get it set up. This year, Dad has already been out on the snowmobile, and he found a nice cedar tree. It is set up now, sparkling with icicles and ornaments.

The horses are near the house, drinking out of the well. Mom rustles the oats in a bucket, and they trail in, first slowly, then running, crowding each other to get the first bite of grain.

The trees we want are up the road about two miles, near the head of a deep draw. The horses break into a trot, covering the snowy ground quickly. I nudge Gazelle into a gallop, and he twists his neck, shakes his head, and acts like a bronc, crowhopping in exuberance. Mom kicks Redwing, and for a moment it's a race across the snowy ground. The snow swirls up from the horses' hooves like ocean spray, and the wind whips at my face.

Taking the distance at a trot and a gallop, it doesn't take us long to reach the cedar grove, and we spook up several cedar waxwings as we ride up. A deer, shaggy in her winter coat, jerks up her head and watches us, big mule ears stiff. Deciding we're harmless, she walks off, snipping at the tall grasses with her teeth.

It's peaceful up here in the draw, smelling the spicy fragrance of cedar and watching the herd of white and tan antelope that trails across the hillside above us, almost invisible against the brown grass and snow.

I hold the horses and let them graze while Mom unties the wood saw from her saddle strings and walks around the trees, cutting off several full, long branches loaded with blue juniper berries. Most of the cedars up this draw are low-growing, bushy trees, reminding me of my favorite cedar on the ranch, which is also a low-growing, bushy tree; it looks like a huge underwater clump of green moss. It clings to a high, rocky point, buffeted by the Wyoming winds. Dad calls it the Woolly Mammoth, and during the hunting season, buck deer are commonly found near it.

Mom finishes cutting the greens and hands some to me to tie on my saddle strings. We carry some in front of us on our saddles as well, and I think of the Christmas card depicting a cowboy carrying a Christmas tree in front of him on a saddle. As Dad usually cuts trees six feet or more tall, carrying one across a saddle seems unpractical and difficult.

There is hot soup for lunch, simmering on the coal stove and beckoning us with its tomato fragrance.

"You doing anything after lunch?" Dad asks me.

"Nope, not that I know of."

"Let's take the snowmobiles and go check the tubs on the ridge in the heifer pasture. Make sure they haven't licked them out yet."

The wind has come up since this morning, and the blue sky is now gray with clouds rolling in from the northwest. The temperature has dropped to ten degrees.

"Better dress warm," Mom warns. I dress in a snowmobile suit and wear heavy leather and sheep wool mittens.

The snowmobiles can reach speeds of up to fifty miles per hour on the level, and the wind chill factor is very high. The windshield on the machines is little protection, but it does help some.

Dad has the snowmobiles out of the garage and running, puffing oily smoke. Dad is riding "Big John," a 440 John Deere machine, the biggest one we have. We have a 300 "Little John," but that wouldn't start today, so Dad has the year-old 340 Spitfire warmed up for me. The snowmobile engine is between my feet, and the heat melts the snow off my overshoes and helps to keep my feet warm. I test the hand throttle and brake to make sure they are working before revving my machine to follow Dad down the county road. The wind hits my face, and Dad's machine throws a

137

spray of stinging snow particles at me. I push harder on the throttle and ride alongside Dad, who isn't going full out.

We turn and go through a pasture gate, bouncing over the drift in the bar pit along the road. Dad opens the gate, closes it again, and sets a fast pace across the field. We stop to go through another gate, then we are in the pasture where Dad wants to check the tubs. Dad follows a snow-buried road, and I follow him. He rides the faster machine and is more adventuresome than I am. I try to dodge the rocks and sage sticking up through the snow, but my runner hits a sagebrush and halfway upsets me. The snow gets down my neck as I flounder to right myself and the machine, then I am off again, trying to stay in Dad's tracks.

Dad leads up the ridge over humps of dirt and around sharp corners. Going up the hill, there is a patch of ice, and my machine spins for a moment before catching hold and going up. Dad waits for me at the top. As I catch up, he is off again, bouncing over sage and dirt clumps.

The snow is starting, tiny flakes making the valleys below us hazy. The mountains are wrapped in the blanket of snowy clouds. Dad rides up to two tubs, and I follow. The tubs are still half full of supplement.

"I wonder if the heifers have found them yet?" I ask Dad.

"I don't know. Maybe not." We put the heifers in this pasture each year to feed them a little extra after their first calf is weaned. A two-year-old heifer is still growing and needs the extra feed for her and her calf. After she has had the second calf, she is considered a cow and goes with the older animals.

"There's some down there. Let's go check them." If we see animals as we are driving or riding around the pastures, we try to take a look at them, especially now, to make sure there are none that have aborted their calves or are sick.

138

The trail down is steep and rough, full of cutbanks and rocks. Dad darts off one cutbank, and I follow, feeling the snowmobile fly through the air then land with a jar that nearly upsets me. There are three of these bone-jarring drops on the way down to the cattle.

The heifers look at us suspiciously, then turn tail and gallop off, bucking and kicking.

"I think they're fine," I yell, and Dad turns his machine back up the hill, making a new trail.

The wind is stronger, swirling the snow around us, blotting out the far ridges. Up on the ridge the wind is bitter cold, and my hands feel numb even inside the heavy mittens. Dad leads the way down the ridge, stopping to check the tubs. I know what trail he plans to take, and I wish he wouldn't.

The road drops steeply off the ridge and wanders down into a deep draw. I ride the brake down the hill, trying not to rear-end Dad's snowmobile. Hitting the level, Dad veers off the road and takes off across the flat.

Now I don't know where he's going, unless he wants to go back to the same gate we came through coming out. In my opinion, the sides of the draw are too rough to go down except on the road, now behind us. Dad doesn't share my opinion; he rides to the edge of the draw and plunges over the edge. I ride up and stop, expecting to see a wreck. Dad is waiting for me, sitting calmly on his machine.

I gulp and slowly follow his tracks down the steep, rough hillside, almost overturning but not quite. I make it to the bottom and try to act nonchalant.

"Nice road," I tell him.

"Yeah. I made that last week. Can't get up it, but you can get down."

Dad sets a more subdued pace going home, and I am glad to get inside near the warm stove, leaving the bitter wind and the snow outside.

139

Christmas is over, the tree is taken down, and the merry paper is turned to ashes. Tonight is cold, with snow lying deep in the pockets of hills and on the pasturelands. It has been cold for several days, and the snow squeaks under my feet. The stars are brilliant overhead, always brighter in the clear winter sky than during the summer. Clouds are boiling up black over the mountains, but in the northern sky there is a faint glow. The landscape gives off a white glow of starlight reflected on white snow. Even without the quarter moon the night would be glowing.

The five Angus heifers that I purchased last week bawl from my corral, wanting more feed. I throw some hay over the fence and go into the barn to get some cake, feeling my way to the electrical light switch. The light clicks on, dazzling my eyes and looking deceptively warm. A black cat comes out of the straw stack in the barn and rubs against me as I pour cow cake from the sack into the bucket. "Hi Black. Chilly tonight, isn't it?" I pet the cat and he purrs, then leaps back up on the straw to curl up for the night.

A warm wind comes up as I feed the cows, a chinook wind, warm southern air that rushes across the western plains melting snow and giving a welcome relief from the cold weather. The warm air steadily raises the temperature; already it is ten degrees or so warmer than it was just two or three minutes ago. The wind whistles around the barn sounding cold but warming the air.

I feed the cows and listen to them eat the hard chunks of cake. The cloud bank over the mountains is rearing into the sky, blotting out the stars. The light in the northern sky is brighter, and it takes on a greenish cast, flickering and waving, dancing on the hilltop. It's the aurora borealis, or northern lights, frequently seen in the northern reaches of the country.

140

The wind whips my hair around my face, sounding like the cold north wind but feeling very warm. The snow in the lower pasture seems to visibly shrink against the onslaught of warm air. The temperature, in this brief fifteen-minute period, has risen from zero to forty degrees with just the warm wind pushing it up. The snow beneath my feet is soft, and the wind feels very dry.

The aurora borealis is adding it's fantastic display to the warm night. The spires of light change from green to white and shoot high into the sky like a jet of water from a fountain. Slowly they fall back, then shoot into the sky again, trying to reach the North Star with long fingers of light. One set shimmers in a red ribbon of light, waving as if pushed by the warm wind.

The chinook wind is whipping the trees around and rattling the loose panes of glass in my windows. The pine tree in back of the house is waving with the wind, its top seeming to brush the night sky. The snow is melting faster, leaving puddles of water and patches of damp brown earth. The pasture is spotted with white snow and brown earth.

The northern lights flicker and fade, the spires falling short of their marks. The sky darkens, and I am alone with the warm wind and the dark, starlit sky. The magic is gone, the night is once again dark and dreary. I go back into the house to wait for Richard.

By morning, the chinook has blown itself out, leaving behind wet ground and a few banks of snow. The day is chilly, and the clouds have moved from the mountains and now cover the sky. It looks stormy, but that is nothing unusual. Often a chinook brings a blizzard in its wake. What snow is left is crusted, making it difficult for cattle to find grass. We will start feeding soon so they can depend on hay instead of digging through the snow.

FEEDING

In the early days of cattle raising in Wyoming, cattle were left to fend for themselves during the winter, and many died of starvation when the snow covered the grass. Cattle, unlike horses, don't paw through the snow for grass but burrow under the snow with their wide noses. When the snow becomes crusted, they cannot reach the grass.

With the price of cattle increasing, and fencing becoming a popular means of restraining livestock, ranchers began to see the advantage to putting up dryland and later alfalfa hay for feed during the deep-snow months. Hay was cut and fed by means of horsedrawn equipment, and some people today still use wagons and teams for feeding.

Most, however, use mechanical equipment—pickups, tractors, and now the hydraulic hay lift equipment designed for the large round or square bales. In addition to the hay, we also feed grain cake to help the cattle get enough nutrients during the winter.

The air is cold this morning; the thermometer reads a shivery twenty below zero. I pull on my down coat as well as a heavy snowmobile suit against the cold and unplug the head bolt heater from the pickup. It takes awhile for the heater to put out warm air, but when it does the heat is welcome.

Inside the ranch house it is too warm for my layers of clothing. "Want a cup of coffee?" Dad asks. Mom, attending college in Ranchester this winter to obtain a degree in theology, has already left.

"Sure. How cold is it out here?" Most of the time it is colder out here than it is at my place.

"It was thirty below at five-thirty. I've been scared to look since."

I check the thermometer just outside the kitchen window. It has warmed up. "It's twenty-five below. It's only twenty below at my place."

"Still too damn cold." Dad pours me a cup of coffee and refills his cup. "We have to load hay today, too."

"We should have done it yesterday. It was warmer." The coffee is hot, black, and strong. Cowboy coffee. As one hunter said, it has "authority." "We have to load cake too, don't we?"

"Yep. I didn't do that either."

The sun is touching the hilltops to the west as we bundle into the heavy snowmobile suits and heavy gloves to step out into the breathtaking cold. Dad starts the pickup and backs it out of the garage while I open the gate and walk to the steel granary where the cake is stored. Dad backs up as I open the door of the granary and jump inside, grabbing the scoop shovel to shovel the cake into the truck.

When Dad gets the pickup close enough, hitting the granary with his trailer hitch, I dig into the pile of cake with my scoop, filling the scoop nearly full. Dad grabs a scoop out of the pickup and joins me, and we work in rhythm. Dad scoops cake while I empty mine into the pickup. We work at the same speed, so we keep out of each other's way. We need twenty scoops, so we each throw on ten. That makes roughly six hundred pounds, enough for the three hundred-odd cattle to eat about two pounds each.

The cake loaded, we jump in the pickup again, and Dad drives to the stackyard to get hay, about four miles up the road. The stackyard is fenced with barbed wire to keep the cattle from getting in and helping themselves. It does little to stop deer, as they bound right over it. There is a stack of the small square bales, left over from last winter, and we will feed these before starting on the large round ones we stacked last summer.

Dad stops and lets me open the gate, then drives through to back up to the stack while I shut the gate. The cows haven't gathered up yet, but they are coming in a long line from across the draw. If we load the hay and feed it first, most should be here in time to get their mouthfuls of cake. I clamber up to the top layer of the haystack to help with the loading. The wind has come up since we left, turning the air even colder.

"Good grief, it's cold." The wind slices through my snowmobile suit.

"It's the wind. Drops the chill factor," Dad says.

"Blasted wind." I survey the snowy landscape from the top of the stack. Wind swirls the snow in tiny cyclones. I grab a bale of hay and toss it down to Dad, who is waiting on the pickup bed. It thuds as it hits, rocking the pickup gently. Dad moves it to the front of the bed, starting the bottom layer.

I grab another bale, but the snow has it frozen in. I tug, and the mice chewed string breaks with a stifled pop. The sudden release unbalances me, and I'm glad I'm not on the edge of the stack where it's easy to tumble off. I reach for another bale, leaving the broken one for another day. The string holds and the bale lands with a dull plunk. The stack on the pickup grows higher. I throw the last bale and and jump from haystack to pickup.

"How long did it take?" I ask. We have a competition going; each day we try to beat the previous day's record.

"Twelve minutes," Dad says, looking at his watch. "Two minutes faster than yesterday."

"We were rolling." I jump off the pickup stack and walk to open the gate, while Dad churns the pickup through the snow. Dad stops and lets me get into the warm cab. The fast work and the warm cab make the sweat run down my face, fogging my glasses. My heavy hat, looking like something out of a Cossak movie, is too hot, but it felt good on the cold haystack.

Dad stops the pickup. "We'll feed down here today."

I pull my hat back on and clamber up on top of the haystack on the pickup. The bales near the edge are wobbly, so I scramble to the middle of the load. It's easy to fall off when the bales give way.

Digging my pocket knife out of my snowmobile suit pocket, I cut the strings on several of the bales along the edge and yell "Ready." Dad moves the pickup forward slowly, and I push the hay off for the hungry cattle, watching them run forward to devour it. Dad swings around in a large circle while I throw off the hay. Finishing, I thump on the pickup roof and he stops, ready to let me drive while he feeds the cake off the tailgate of the pickup.

Smokey, a half-Charolais, comes up expecting her special bite. Although not a pet, Smokey has learned that she can get extra by letting us feed her by hand. I grab a handful of cake out of the pickup and she takes it eagerly, wrapping her tongue around my hand.

145

"Just like feeding a thrashing machine," Dad says, giving her another handful.

I jump into the pickup and drive slowly while Dad feeds off the cake. "Okay," he calls as he finishes.

Dad gets back in the cab and drives across the county road to the reservoir. During the cold weather we have to chop water so the cattle can drink. Stopping on the hill above the pond, Dad looks at me. "You chop."

I find the axe buried under hay stems and head to the pond, slipping and sliding on the icy trail. The wheatfields above me, waiting for next spring to be seeded in wheatgrass, are spotted white and brown. The hills rising up from them are snow covered; they almost blend in with the pale sky.

The ice flies up and hits my face as the axe bites into it. I move around the hole, not chopping deep enough yet to hit water but deep enough to leave a trail around the outer edge of the water hole. The hole is about two feet in diameter, and I hope to chop it so that the ice will come out in one big slab instead of small chunks. I chop around the hole three times, then chop deep enough so water sprays up on my face, forming ice crystals and then melting with my body heat. Before long, the axe head is white with ice. The chunk comes free, and I pull it out, smelling the black mud and stale water. The ice is thick, around two inches. The bottom is black with mud, but inside it is crystal clear, making rainbows. Now the cattle can water, and I suspect the deer take advantage of the open water as well.

Today, we have to feed on the place we lease near Buffalo. During the summer we raise hay, and a neighbor does the haying in return for half of the hay. The arrangement works well, and Dad and Bernard don't have to run up during the summer to do the hay work.

The weaned calves are trucked up here in the fall, where they have open water in Clear Creek all winter. Every other day we drive the thirty miles to feed them hay and cake and

146

to check the mineral mix that we feed them free choice. Free choice rations are mixed with salt to make sure the cattle won't eat too much. They'll naturally limit their own salt intake.

It's a nice day. The cold broke last night, the sun is shining, and the temperature is around ten above. The calves are waiting for us when we get to Buffalo, and Dad blows the pickup horn to call in any stragglers. The calves learn to come to the horn and never forget it. Go into any pasture, blow a pickup horn, and cattle come from all over, hoping for food.

The calves are trailing in from all corners of the pasture, thinking of hay and cake. Dad lets me drive while he shovels out cake in a long, narrow trail. The calves crowd and push to get at the cake, and soon there is a single line of calves behind the pickup, heads down, looking like a huge part in a head of brown hair. Dad motions for me to stop, and he gets in on the passenger side.

"Drive over to the mineral tubs, and we'll pour out this mineral mix," Dad says. This mix is different from the molasses stuff. This is composed of several minerals in a mixture of crushed grains. It is poured into wooden feeders and has a texture like fine sand. The feeders are not far from the creek, and along the banks are piles of deep snow.

"There's a yearling. Looks like he's stuck," I tell Dad.

The calf is stuck. He was heading for water and got into snow too deep for his short legs. He is trapped in the snow.

"Stupid calf," Dad comments.

I'm inclined to agree. There are several well-worn trails to the water; why dive off into a snowbank?

"I wish I had a rope," Dad says, wading out into the snow. I follow, sinking into the snow and wallowing around. The calf struggles as he sees us coming but can't go far. He shows his fear by bellowing and rolling his eyes. Dad gets close to him and tries to spook him out of the snow. The calf

147

lunges and fights harder to get away. Dad jumps at him, waist deep in the snow. I yell and wave my arms. The calf struggles again, then finds solid ground. He leaps out and runs back to the rest of the herd.

"Good thing we found him," Dad says, wading out of the drift.

We carry the mineral sacks to the feeders and pour the mineral in.

Dad drives back to the haystack so we can load the first load of hay. Instead of being on the stack, I have to stack the hay in the pickup bed this time, in my opinion a harder job. I am just getting the first bale lined up when Dad throws another down. I grab it and manhandle it into place beside the first one. The bottom layers are easy, but as the stack on the pickup grows, it gets harder to push and heave the bales up.

The bales are placed in alternating rows, the bottom ones lying on edge, placed parallel to the pickup bed. We load eleven on this bottom layer, putting four on the open tailgate. The next layer is transverse of the pickup, to make the load more stable. In this way, we can haul up to 60 bales.

We have to feed two loads of 60 bales each, then we load up 40 to take home for our livestock there. The calves eat the hay greedily, but 120 bales should be enough hay for two days. It is almost noon by the time we finish and head home. The work makes us thirsty, so when Dad suggests a beer stop at Ucross, I have no objections. I ask for a glass of water first and then order a Coors Light. We try our luck at the dice shake; if you get two of a kind, you can win a free drink. Dad has all the luck, shaking out a four of a kind and winning a sixpack.

"Not bad," I tell him, walking out. "Buy two get six free."

"Well, almost. We had to each put in a quarter for a shake."

148

"Six for fifty cents then."

"You'll have to feed the heifers by yourself tomorrow," Dad says, remembering he has to go meet with the book- keeper in Buffalo.

I get to the ranch around eight, but Dad has already left. We loaded the hay yesterday afternoon, and the loaded pickup is waiting for me in the garage. I have to feed cattle in two pastures—those in the Bailey place and the heifers in the creek pasture. There aren't too many in the Bailey place, but there are about a hundred in the creek pasture.

I check the water in the water tank and chop a hole for the cattle. They come stringing in, wanting feed. I throw off three bales of hay, cut the strings, and kick the hay around before driving forward a few yards to throw out three more. I only have to feed twelve bales here, so this method will work well. To feed the fifty bales left, I plan to use another method.

When we were kids, the men used to put the pickup in extra low and let us steer the pickup while they fed. Our legs were too short to reach the gas, so it was a good system. You can also take a piece of baler twine, tie the steering wheel to the gear shift, and let the pickup go.

I find a piece of twine behind the seat and tie the wheel short enough to keep it from turning the pickup too much. Setting the gears in extra low, I let the clutch out slowly and jump out while the pickup is moving. It's going very slowly, so I can crawl into the back and onto the bales. I watch the road ahead while I'm throwing off hay, and I see the pickup gather speed as it heads toward a deep draw. The string was too long. I jump out and run to the cab, jumping in and braking the pickup before it can run away. I drive it back to the road, aiming it uphill this time, and tie the string shorter. Jumping on back, I start feeding again only to have the pickup come to a sudden halt, almost knocking me off. The pickup has hit a ditch and can't go fast enough to get

149

through. I try again, and this time the pickup moves along at a slow pace, and I can feed off the remaining hay. The cattle investigate the hay, then leave it, wanting cake. After I feed the cake they will eat the hay, but they don't want to miss anything.

My invisible driver does quite well now, and I can shovel off the cake without worrying about running into a draw. So far, the pickup has never run away with anyone doing this, but there is always a chance.

I finish by 11 A.M., and I'm glad to go home and have a light lunch of soup and sandwiches and curl up with a good book.

WINTER CHORES

Winter chores include lots of things, such as bringing in sick cows and doctoring them, making sure that  calving heifer are in near the buildings, and checking the livestock to make sure they are wintering well.

At times we have to ride out and bring cattle that are trapped by deep snow into the feed grounds, or bring in early calves that might die during the cold weather or snowstorms.

"Can you feed the cake by yourself this morning? I have to go into Buffalo with Bernard to see the banker to sign something. We shouldn't be gone too long."

"Sure," I agree. Bernard follows us to the turn into our land, then Dad jumps out and rides with him, turning the pickup over to me.

I drive around the pasture, honking the horn. Down on the icy creek, I see a group of calves drinking out of a ripple. As I wait, one slips off the ice and into the water. His head bobs up and down with the waves, and he tries to lunge out, but his feet keep slipping on the ice. Ever since the other day, when we found the calf in the snowbank, Dad has been carrying a rope behind the pickup seat. I find it and slide down the bank onto the ice. Getting the rope around the calf's neck is no problem, but I'm not sure how I can pull him out. He weighs around 400 pounds to my 140.

He tries to jump out, and I pull on the rope, but he fights the unfamiliar pressure on his neck. I try to just pull him, but he's too heavy. He swims across the ripple, but the other side is too deep for him to get a foothold.

I wish Dad and Bernard would hurry up, but I don't hear a pickup engine anywhere. I'm afraid if I leave him, he'll be swept under the ice and drown.

The calf swims back to me, and I try to reach into the icy water and grab his front legs. If I can lift them out of the water onto the ice, maybe he can get out. But he won't let me get a hold on his legs and keeps swimming away.

I reach down and take the rope off his neck, thinking that maybe I can drive the pickup close enough to tie the rope to it and pull him out that way. But I find I can't drive the pickup close enough, because of the steep bank. The rope falls short by several feet. I'll have to try to do it alone.

I need to get the rope behind his front shoulder to keep him from fighting when the rope tightens. When it's around his neck, it chokes him, and he pulls away. I make a large loop and drop it into the water, waiting for the calf to swim through it. He does, and I can see that one front leg and his head are through the rope. I take up the slack and pull the calf toward me.

The calf is nearly done in. His legs float out from his body with the motion of the water. He can't take too much more before hypothermia sets in. I have to get him out soon. There is still no sign of Dad and Bernard.

Near me is an ice shelf under the water, about three feet down. If the calf can stand on that, it might give him the resistance he needs to get out, with me pulling on the rope. The calf stands beside me, his head resting on the ice. If he gives up, there is little I can do.

He feels the ice under his hooves and makes a weak attempt to jump out. "Come on, baby," I mutter, pulling on the rope. I keep it taut, giving him the extra help he needs. He folds his front legs, hitting the ice with his knees. I pull on the rope. The calf struggles weakly, worn out from the cold and the swimming. I back up slowly, keeping the rope taut, not wanting him to slip back into the water now. His back is out, then his hips and hind legs are out. He stands, trembling with cold. His ankles are so cold they won't straighten, and he walks with his hooves bent under. I grab the rope and take it off his neck while he is still too cold to move fast. As I coil it up again, I hear Dad and Bernard coming down the road.

I walk up to their pickup. "I had to pull a calf out of the creek. I think he'll be okay."

"We're apt to lose some this year," Dad says.

"Maybe we can move them to the other waterhole, up the creek. Have you fed them yet?" Bernard asks.

"No."

154

We call the calves and they follow the pickup up the creek. From now on we'll feed them here and hope that no more will fall into the creek.

It's warm again today, and after we feed Dad says, "Let's go up in the horse pasture and see if we can find that white horse. He wasn't with the others this morning."

We drive on into the pasture. All the horses are there except Silver. It is unusual for a horse to be very far from the others, so we worry if they aren't all there. Dad drives up the road that leads to the ridge. We call it the petrified forest road—down off the ridge along the road are several petrified trees. There's a deep snowbank across the road, and it takes Dad two tries to get through it. Many times we can't. We check the draw along the road but see no white horse grazing on the winter-dry grass.

"He could have gotten caught in the fence," I mutter, watching the fence line closely. One of our horses caught a foot in the wire once and stood waiting patiently for help to come. We drive along the ridge, checking all the fence lines. Still no sign of Silver.

"Maybe I'd better go out on horseback and look for him." I am thinking of all that can happen to horses on the range. He could have caught his foot in some old, buried wire and be waiting for help. He could have slipped and broken a leg, as a friend's horse did. He was gentle and easy to catch; someone might have stolen him. Or he could be dead.

We cover all the country we can in the pickup, then we head back home. Mike and Linda Sue are down from Ranchester for the weekend, so I invite Mike to ride along, knowing he rode Silver over the summer.

"Ride careful," Dad warns us as we saddle up. "It's pretty slick out for barefoot horses." He means horses that

155

are not shod with sharp shoes made especially for icy riding conditions.

"We'll mostly walk." I'm a veteran of several horse wrecks, so I take few chances.

Gazelle leads the way, and Mike follows on Redwing, lamenting that she's not as fast as Silver. Mom likes Redwing though, even if she is slow. Mom is in Sheridan today, or she would enjoy a ride. The fence pliers flop on my saddle, and the pistol weighs heavy on my belt. Fence pliers in case he's caught in wire, the pistol in case he broke a leg and we have to shoot him. I hope we don't have to use it.

We checked the fence line this morning in the pickup, so from the horses we mostly plan to check the draws, making sure he is not down in one, out of sight from the road. The first draw is empty except for cottontail rabbits, who scatter as we approach. Following the draw to it's head, we ride up the swale where Dad and I almost wedged the pickup between two rocks last summer. We check each branch of the draw carefully, but no horse.

We ride across the road, down into another draw and back out, over a ridge and into another one. Still nothing but deer, rabbits, and brush.

"I wonder if someone stole him?" I wonder aloud. It seems doubtful that they would steal just one horse, but you never know.

We have one more draw to check before heading home. Mike, behind me, calls out something. I pull up Gazelle and wait for him to ride alongside.

"I just remembered something. Yesterday morning I heard some strange noises coming from over this way. Like something bellowing. I wonder if it was the horse."

"Could have been. Where at?"

Mike points to the draw we haven't checked yet, a deep, rough draw that one friend thought would have made a good buffalo jump. It's deep enough that a fall would kill a horse

156

if it dropped over the edge. The drop is seventy-five to one hundred feet straight down.

"If he fell in here, he's gone," I comment, riding down the pickup tracks to the rim of the draw.

Gazelle acts nervous, his ears jerking back and forth, and he refuses to walk up to the edge of the draw. I dismount and lead him, better able to see into the draw. One fork is empty, but at the head of the other fork I can see a gray-white tail. Walking closer, I can see Silver's body, lying at the foot of the dropoff.

"He's here, Mike. He must have fallen off. Another horse probably dived at him to bite him, and he jumped over." I watch the carcass for any sign of life, but the big head doesn't lift to watch us, and the rounded side is still, with no sign of breathing. The ears are still, and the eyes are closed. It looks like there is a humped up mound of frozen dirt under his body. He probably fell on that, breaking several ribs. The snow by his mouth is red, a sign of internal bleeding.

"Darn fighting horses," I mutter. I hate to see a dead horse, especially when the death is as useless as this one. I lead Gazelle away from the draw and mount, thankful that the cold, still body is not his. We have been together for seventeen years, and I'll miss him when he's gone.

"I'll bet you feel bad," I mention to Mike. "You rode him a lot and kinda liked him."

"Yeah, it shakes you up a little. He was a good horse to ride."

I feel a little shaken, but on a ranch these things happen. You have to keep things in perspective and accept them. Cows, horses, calves, and pets die, sometimes needlessly. If you can't learn to live with it, you shouldn't be in the business.

157

Riding back, we see Dad coming up the county road in the pickup, checking the well to make sure the water is running. I let Gazelle trot over the icy ground to the fence.

"Find him?" Dad asks.

"Yeah. We found him dead, in that draw just across the ridge."

"I figured something like that. Want to unsaddle and ride back in the pickup?"

It isn't far to the house, but the sun is getting low in the west, and the evening chill is creeping up. Dad's offer sounds good. We strip off tack and turn the horses loose, climbing into the warm pickup cab.

"That leaves us short of horses," I mention. Dad sold Lucy last summer, so that leaves us with Redwing, Gazelle, Dynamite, and Catawba.

"We've got a horse apiece," Dad says.

"Since the ice has melted, let's take the horses out and move some of those cattle from the Charlie Francis place into the Devo country," Dad says. We have already done the morning feeding on this February day, and Dad has been talking about moving a few of the cattle out of the Charlie Francis place for some time. Today looks like a good day.

We corral the horses and give them a feed of oats, then eat our own lunch before getting ready to go. Gazelle prances eagerly, wanting to get this job over with so he can get back to eating.

Near the well in the Charlie Francis place are most of the cattle, including one that has a prolapse. A prolapse is caused when a cow's muscles don't hold the uterus firmly in place, and it protrudes. It is a common ailment in Hereford cows and normally occurs before or after calving. We will have to get her in and call Bernard to come down and push the prolapse back, then sew the cow up to avoid a repeat. The cow isn't far from the gate, so we ease the horses around her and slowly herd her down the road and through the gate.

158

Now she is in the home pasture and will be easier to find to-morrow when Bernard can doctor her.

Shutting the gate, we ride back and cut off about forty-five head of cattle to move out of this pasture. There should only be fifty cows in a pasture this size, and at last count we had around one hundred here. There isn't enough pasture for that many cows. Dad rides ahead to open the gate into the next pasture, and the cows trail down the road and through the gate as if they knew where they were going.

"Good job," Dad says, watching the cattle spread out to eat. "Now we'll get the prolapse into the corral."

The cow was easy to handle when we drove her through the gate into this pasture, and she trots out well until she sees the corral gate, open ahead of her. She turns back and runs up the draw toward the pasture she just left. Dad gallops down to head her, but she doubles back, quicker than his horse, and runs up the fence line. Dad and I kick our horses into a gallop to head her, hoping to use the fence line to block one side. The cow runs faster, but the horses outrun her and block her escape. She heads to the corral again, then cuts off and jumps down into a deep ditch that runs through the pasture. She disappears for a moment, then reappears on the other side, heading back to the Charlie Francis place at a run.

"Leave her," Dad says. "If we push her, she's apt to go through the fence. We'll get her tomorrow after she calms down."

The next day is Saturday, and Mom turns out to help us. With the three of us surrounding her, the cow doesn't have much choice and goes into the corral before she can change her mind. Dad called Bernard last night, and he is waiting in the corral. I take the horses up and strip off sad-dles, then go back to the corral to see if I can help.

"Cynthy, can you find me some Lysol?" Bernard asks.

I go back to the house and mix some Lysol with warm water to be used as a disinfectant, then I take the bucket of mix back to the corral. The cow is in the squeeze chute, and Bernard is waiting for me so he can doctor her. The cow is red-eyed and nasty tempered when they open the head gate and let her out. Dad opens the head gate and is sent up the fence by a charging cow. The cow then spies Bernard and lets out an angry grunt. She runs at him head down, neck stiff. Bernard jumps up on the fence, out of range.

"Cynthy, jump down behind the gate and swing your hat at her. I'd like to put her in the other corral."

I wonder why I didn't leave while the leaving was good. Still, I'm in the best position, as I am on the fence between the two corrals. I work my way down the poles and get behind the green panel gate. I take off my woolly hat and stick it through the bars of the gate, waving it around in the opening between the two corrals. If the cow charges at it, she should go right through the gate, and I can safely swing it shut behind her. The cow sees the movement and charges, her momentum carrying her through the gate. I quickly shut the panel gate and latch it securely before she can turn and come back.

Bernard gathers up his doctoring equipment and remarks that the cow probably won't live anyway, as the prolapsed uterus is bleeding so much. He's right. Two hours later the cow is stretched out on her side, dead. Dad and I take the tractor down and hook chains to her stiffening legs and drag her away from the buildings.

EPILOGUE

Today is spring. The sun is out, and the cool breeze smells of spring grass and rain. I ride Gazelle up on a low ridge and pull up, enjoying the panorama of hills and valleys. Ahead of me I can see the blue Big Horn Mountains, the snow on the high peaks gleaming white in the sun.

 The valley to the north of me is shadowed by storm clouds, and I can see a rainstorm moving up the valley, borne by the wind. The hills are gray and blurry with rain, and it curtains the valley as it moves south.

The sun hides, wrapped in the woolly gray cloud. The rain hits suddenly, the wind slashing it around us. Gazelle turns his back to the rain, and we stand, letting the cold spring rain wash over us, turning his chestnut coat to a dark brown.

The wind, colder now, pushes the shower past, sweeping it down the valley toward the broken hills of the Powder River country. The hills turn misty as the rain sweeps over them.

The sun throws off the cloud blanket, turning the day back into spring. I nudge Gazelle gently in the ribs and head toward a little bunch of cattle.

The cattle watch us warily, wondering if it's time to move. Today I am just checking them, making sure there are no bum calves or sick cows. Everything looks good—the cows are fat, and the calves are frisky.

There is a rainbow above, brilliant strands of red, green, yellow, and violet arching across the sky, nodding to the sun. Ahead of me, on the green pasturelands, I can see where the rainbow touches the earth for a brief conversation. The rainbow's end, or it's beginning?

I look up, following the arch across the sky with my eyes, seeing where it touches down again behind the ridges.

The rainbow shimmers in the grasses, the colors faint. I turn Gazelle so I can ride through it, and I can see the colors glimmering against my body and getting lost in Gazelle's mane.

Gazelle is unaware of the rainbow, but I pull him up, watching the colors dance around me, feeling privileged to be among them. The colors in the grass grow fainter, melting in the sunlight.

There is supposed to be a pot of gold here at the rainbow's end. I see no pot of gold, glittering and shining. I do see spring grasses, green and lush. I see the white-faced cattle, tiny calves, and barren, brown hillsides. I see the high, blue sky, with the ghost of the rainbow arching over sagebrush-dotted hills and pasturelands. I feel the freedom of the open range and of life and work in the open air. I feel the horse between my knees and know that Nature and I are in close partnership. And I know there is a good God, who allows me to live the way I choose.

This is my pot of gold, my rainbow's end.